2022

CHRISTMAS

with

Southern Living

2022
CHRISTMAS
with Southern Living

INSPIRED IDEAS FOR HOLIDAY
COOKING AND DECORATING

Southern Living BOOKS

CONTENTS

That most wonderful time of the year is here again!

We are thrilled to share the magical locations, inspired decorations, and delicious recipes in this year's edition with you. After months of planning, cooking, propping, styling, and photographing, it is always exciting to hold the finished book in hand. It took quite a team to make it all happen, and we hope you find inspiration with each turn of the page.

Special thanks to those who opened their doors and allowed us to deck their halls, like Sara Kate and Jason Little, proprietors of the historic Bradford House, a restored 1912 home that they have creatively reimagined into a glamorous boutique hotel in the heart of Oklahoma City. The colorful halls, bustling parlors, elegant dining rooms, and cozy guest rooms provide the striking backdrops for the "All Is Bright" story on page 12. Much gratitude to Jan Miller for letting us inside her tiny jewel box of a home perched high on a hill in Birmingham, Alabama, to use as the setting for our "A Cottage Christmas" story on page 34. It is a perfect example of how even the smallest spaces can make a major impression when it comes to stylish living and decorating.

Of course, no edition of this book would be complete without stunning tablescapes and mouthwatering recipes for every occasion, course, and schedule. Whether you have time to cook all day or need something on the table in minutes, the *Southern Living* Test Kitchen experts create dishes that are guaranteed to work and wow your crowd. From the big holiday feast to an intimate family game night, we've got a season of festive menus covered.

Bon appétit and a very merry Christmas to all!

Katherine Cobbs
EXECUTIVE EDITOR

Decorate

A HOLIDAY LOOKBOOK

All Is Bright

Decorating with a kaleidoscope of colors makes a bold statement, especially at Christmastime. Whimsical accents with a retro nod complement the vibrant walls and dramatic rooms of Oklahoma City's historic Bradford House. Owners Jason and Sara Kate Little renovated and reimagined the home as a boutique hotel with a storied past that offers next-level hospitality.

Bike Bells Ring...

Southerners rarely require a sleigh to get around during the holidays, but bicycles with baskets are a fun way to see the sights and Christmas lights. Take a cue from the Bradford House: When you host guests, plan outings with a tourist's eye. Go sightseeing, but leave the car behind. Pedaling your way to the flower market, tree lot, or neighborhood café is the sort of outdoor adventure guaranteed to leave a lasting impression.

Tinsel and Tassels

A vintage cubby in the hotel's entry gets heavy use—tasseled room keys and letters to Santa are picked up daily!—so it makes sense to dress it up in holiday style with frosty bottlebrush trees and blushing pepperberry branches. More tassels in the varied green and blue hues pulled from the room are repeated in the garland that graces the striking Chippendale banister leading to the guest rooms upstairs.

Opposite: To give the hotel a world-traveler aesthetic, Sara Kate commissioned talented British muralist Louise Dean to paint the fanciful Chinoiserie-inspired wall treatment as a nod to elements that the original owners might have brought back to the home from a grand tour to exotic places.

16

Lovely Branches

A seating area in the entry offers guests and visitors a place to sit, meet, or wait for a seat in the bar or dining room. Using ornaments in the same cool color scheme as the room is a fresh, monochromatic approach that adds just enough sparkle. Silver pieces from the owners' collection are shimmering planters for a tiny forest of trees made from cut branches—juniper, fir, and foxtail fern—sprouting from moss-covered floral foam.

Hanging of the Green

The mantel's architectural details shine through unadorned rings and swaths of greenery draped with satin ribbons. Crisp white tulipiere vases and brass candlesticks are the only other ornamentation, unless you count the midcentury Italian Stilnovo chandelier reflected in the mirror. Sara Kate turned to the historical color palettes of Patrick Baty's Papers and Paints in the U.K. for the colors used throughout the house, proving that historical and traditional does not have to equal dated and neutral.

Opposite: A collection of Penguin Classics books with juicy orange covers draws the eye to the scarab blue Drawing Room shelves with a wintry Christmas village tucked inside.

Merry and Bright

The punch-stained color of the Bradford House's Lantern Room has been a draw since the hotel opened its doors. Surprisingly, men request the rosy paint-color formula most often. The balance of warm and cool tones is a cocooning canvas for anything—abstract art, animal prints, and a towering Christmas tree. Waterfalls of ribbon in every shade spill between vintage Shiny Brite ornaments that the Littles have collected over the years.

22

Baby It's Cold Outside

Like the Lantern Room, the bar has magnetic appeal. Sumptuous leather club chairs, velvet barstools, and a captivating lacquered shelf above the bar make it a place to linger. Sara Kate's Pastiche Studios stumbled upon the intricately carved shelf on eBay. It was a closet-surround in a bedroom in an old Pennsylvania Victorian in its previous incarnation. Captivated by its rustic pineapple carvings—a symbol of hospitality—Sara Kate knew the piece was meant for the Bradford House. Vignettes composed of flowers, fruit, and decorative accents are woven between bottles and glasses to add interest throughout the year.

Opposite: A massive wreath hung from an antique mirror by a silk sash provides an elegant focal point in the room during afternoon tea time.

Stockings Were Hung

Brass champagne buckets serve as vases for striking floral displays. Loose bunches of pepperberry, lush white peonies, towering amaryllis, bold anemones, and eucalyptus are long-lasting choices. A decorative brass-rimmed mirror adorned with greenery adds holiday cheer.

Opposite: The French coat hooks that line the chair rail next to the café's swinging service door usually corral staff aprons, but when December comes, a row of stockings in Sister Parish fabrics takes their place. Vintage photos found in scrapbooks in the attic during renovations were framed to create a gallery wall rooted in the home's history and serve to highlight the generations who likely passed through its halls.

At Your Service

When the weather permits, the outdoor terrace provides a bright and airy gathering place for hotel guests and locals alike. Magnolia leaves, flowers, and lush evergreen wreaths soften the marble and cast-iron console created in Lyon, France, from architectural salvage pieces. As if plucked from a patisserie, it is the perfect serving station for a holiday dessert party.

Cheers to the Season

Glasses of bubbly, colorful macarons, and homemade sweets from the hotel's
Quincy Bakeshop are irresistible. Mini Champagne bottles, given a hand-painted
holiday treatment by The Merriment Mill, are festive parting favors for guests
to take home. A mass of peonies, amaryllis, and anemones are the "thriller" in a
footed brass champagne bucket, while seeded eucalyptus and magnolia leaves
provide the "spiller" and "filler" in a perfectly balanced arrangement.

To All a Good Night

Graceful greenery frames the doors and embellishes brass and crystal sconces that light the way to the hotel's upstairs gues trooms. It's another special touch that makes out-of-town guests feel like they are staying in a festively decorated home for the holidays. Rich green velvet headboards are a cozy year-round fixture, but the casual grouping of mirrors above gets gussied up with silk ribbon accents for a dose of fa la la this time of year.

Opposite: Striking architectural details like the chair rail and crown molding gracing Bradford House's Tiffany blue walls are like pretty ribbons wrapping the corridors that lead to the hotel's guest suites.

A Cottage Christmas

In a diminutive shingled cottage nestled on a hilltop in Birmingham, Alabama, unexpected doses of lavender are woven in with the timeless blue and white accents found in the collections and textiles used in the interior. It's a fresh, elegant approach to holiday decorating that lends grandeur to this jewel box of a home.

Festive Focal Points

Homeowner Jan Miller treats the concrete urn in the knot garden just outside her front door like the dining room table centerpiece she doesn't have the space for indoors. She swaps in new elements with each season for a bold first impression.

Opposite: A tiny tree reflected in an antique mirror rises high from a console to make a grand statement. A wicker basket takes the place of the usual tree skirt.

Touches of Jolly

Step inside the front door of Jan's home, designed by architect Bill Ingram, and it's easy to see how stylish small-space living can be. An upholstered banquette does double-duty as seating for dining and a cozy spot to visit. It backs up to the antique ship's galley kitchen tucked out of sight just behind. Rich wood tones and muted greens and blues are a pretty backdrop for the heather hues of the holiday accents woven in throughout the room.

38

Doses of Whimsy

No one would know that a cooktop hides beneath the large silver tray on the campaign-style kitchen cabinet. Jan enlists the tray for serving and as a decorating opportunity. Silver goblets, trophies, and heirloom porcelain pieces hold fruit, flowers, and greenery. Her table seats four for tea or supper, but most often its used like a sideboard for serving cocktail hour nibbles or sweet holiday treats.

Opposite: Plate racks corral dishes and showcase whimsical waves of greenery and tiny stockings,

Cozy Comforts and Holiday Dreams

Greenery, wreaths, and a vase of flowers dress up Jan's bathroom, providing a festive focal point from the marble shower that goes from indoor to outdoor when the weather permits by opening a wall of French doors to the private garden.

Opposite: The motif on the linen fabric framing the window and bed is repeated in a simple boxwood wreath hung from taffeta ribbon above a bedside writing desk and carved faux bois chair.

Sweet Surprises

Stockings with surprises tucked inside grace a sliding ladder on the beds in the bunkroom where Jan's grandchildren stay when they come for a visit. It's a well-appointed room with its shelves of books, reading nook, and wall of framed vintage silhouettes. Opposite the bunks, a series of storybook illustrations with surround a carved stag's head from Germany fitted with real antlers and a garland of lacy evergreens.

Opposite: A Moravian star pendant lights the room like the star on top of a Christmas tree.

A Beautiful Sight...Happy Tonight

In another room, a king-size velvet headboard flanks a queen-size bed turned sideways for an oversize daybed that sleeps two adults or four of Jan's young grandchildren. A garland gracing the top of the bed and a cluster of ornaments dangling from the reading light are pretty touches this time of year.

Opposite: In the hall, Jan decorates an antique painted cabinet that holds a collection of majolica with garland, budding paperwhites, mini poinsettias, and a forest of tiny trees.

Keep It Simple

At the far end of Jan's backyard
is a storage shed where she
keeps seasonal decor, pieces
for entertaining, and garden
tools. It also can be enlisted as
an outdoor bar in a pinch with
the doors flung open and a table
nestled across the threshold.
Because it's a focal point in
the yard, it gets spiffed up with
wreaths, a tree, cool-season
plantings, and hurricanes with
flickering pillar candles.

Mix and Mingle

Moving to a tiny cottage required Jan to pare down her belongings to just those things she loved the very most. She isn't afraid to bring out the fine china and silver to mix with wicker and weathered wood. Mixing things up gives the table patina and interest, and makes any gathering feel like a special occasion.

Opposite: Jan had the expansive table built to host large crowds. It spans the entire length of yard from her awning-covered patio seating area to the storage shed beyond.

Take a Bough

Leave the tangle of Christmas lights in the attic. Sometimes the most striking holiday displays are those that rely on the unparalleled beauty of the seasonal elements that Mother Nature provides—evergreen branches, berries, blossoms, and fruit. Whether you take cuttings from the landscape or visit the flower market, lovely accents like these will last for weeks.

Magnificent Magnolia

The iconic glossy foliage of the Southern magnolia is a holiday standard in garlands, wreaths, and centerpieces. Whether you incorporate the leaves into decor indoors or out, it's best to mist them regularly with water, especially if they're in direct sunlight. If any elements like flowers or fruit fade, swap them out with fresh ones. After the holidays, everything but the ribbons may be composted.

Graceful Garland

Two faux Fraser fir garlands act like wreath forms on the banister, providing structure for wiring the fresh magnolia leaves and dried hydrangea blossoms, spray-painted gold, into a lush display. Waterfalls of lavender ribbon camouflage zip ties used to secure the garlands while adding even more drama to the elegant display.

Diminutive Displays

Think beyond the vase. Turn to julep cups or crystal goblets for tiny arrangements that add
a bit of cheer to even the most unexpected places. Pinecones stand in for flowers as the filler
in this bouquet that includes a mix of fresh clippings.

Opposite: Pretty posies on every plate are a striking change of pace from the usual centerpiece
on the table. Bundle the leaves so that both fronts and backs show for added interest.

Tiny Touches

Shift into neutral with a simple bouquet that incorporates muted colors and a mix of textures. Cedar, spiral eucalyptus, dusty miller, and a branch holding a trio of petite pinecones create the look above that adds unexpected charm to a bookshelf, bedside table, or windowsill. Add a fragrant evergreen "tassel" to stockings, or use it as a pretty embellishment for cabinet knobs or chair backs. Contrasting textures of magnolia leaves, cypress, pine, and eucalyptus provide a pretty backdrop for a spray of bright red berries.

Opposite: Petite wreaths come together in a snap. A few sprigs of pine, rosemary, or cypress wired together and tied with bows can dress up a coffee table, embellish a gift, or be used as napkin rings on the table.

Special Deliveries

Sure, gift wrap can be pretty, but the real key to showstopping packages is what's on top. Up your gifting game by layering satin or velvet ribbon with burlap or twine. Take presents to designer status by incorporating natural accents like cuttings from your Christmas tree, woodsy herb bundles, cinnamon sticks, or dried fruit. Forego writing "To" and "From" directly on packages and use pretty tags instead.

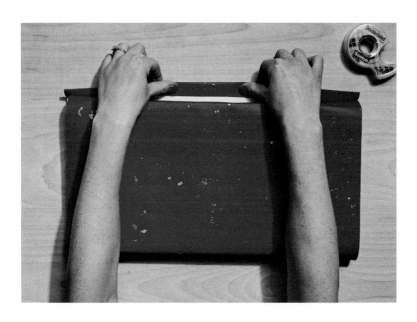

Wrap Like a Pro

Master these three secrets for polished presents every time.

Top: Measure Paper Properly. Place box atop gift wrap, and pull opposite sides of paper around it. Make sure all sides are covered with a 2-inch overlap before cutting.

Middle: Make Things Seamless. Fold one side of the paper up slightly over one edge of the box. Bring opposite side around gift so where the edges meet aligns with the corner of the box.

Bottom: Mask Any Imperfections. Fold the exposed edge under half an inch to hide uneven cuts. Apply double-sided tape to the underside of the paper, and press down firmly.

Entertain

HOLIDAY MENUS

Board Meetings

The season for gathering is here, and the ways to celebrate are as limitless as your imagination. Food boards have moved beyond standard meats and cheeses. Whether brunch is your favorite way to entertain or cocktail hour is your specialty, serving things on an abundant food board is a fresh approach to the usual get-together. It's as easy as whipping up a few from-scratch recipes and combining them with store-bought ingredients for memorable feasts tailor-made for mingling.

APPALACHIAN BREAKFAST BOARD CREOLE BRUNCH BOARD

FLORIBBEAN SUNSET BOARD DELTA DESSERT BOARD

The Appalachian Breakfast Board

Delight your crowd with an abundant board loaded with breakfast favorites inspired by the hills and hollers of Appalachia. Buttermilk biscuits can be slathered with sorghum butter or tangy-sweet apple butter, smothered in sausage gravy, or eaten with country ham. A mix of make-ahead and quick recipes like tater tot skewers combined with purchased ingredients makes this spread easy on the host.

MAKE

BABY BUTTERMILK BISCUITS WITH SORGHUM BUTTER (RECIPE P. 70)

SPECKLED SAUSAGE GRAVY (RECIPE P. 70)

TATER TOT SKEWERS (RECIPE P. 71)

SLOW-COOKER APPLE BUTTER (RECIPE P. 71)

BUY

COUNTRY HAM (SLICED)

PLAIN GREEK YOGURT

HONEY

BLACKBERRIES

RASPBERRIES

GRANOLA

DRINK

Chocolate Coffee: Place ¾ cup semisweet chocolate chips in a 12-cup coffee pot. Brew 12 cups coffee over the chocolate. Remove pot and stir to incorporate melted chocolate. Return pot to burner to keep warm for serving. Serve with whipped cream and cinnamon sticks, if desired.

Baby Buttermilk Biscuits with Sorghum Butter

MAKES **18 TO 20 BISCUITS** ACTIVE **25 MIN.** TOTAL **50 MIN.**

By scaling traditional buttermilk biscuits down to a smaller size, guests can enjoy them in different ways—with pats of sorghum butter, a spoonful of apple butter, slices of country ham, or a scoop of sausage gravy. Split the biscuits before arranging them on the board to make slathering or filling easy.

1/2 cup (4 oz.) cold vegetable shortening or butter

2 1/2 cups (13 3/4 oz.) self-rising flour

1 cup chilled whole buttermilk

Parchment paper

2 Tbsp. butter, melted

Sorghum Butter (recipe follows)

1. Preheat oven to 475°F. Cut cold shortening into flour with a pastry cutter in a medium bowl. Chill 10 minutes.

2. Make a well in center of mixture. Add buttermilk; stir 15 times. Dough will be sticky.

3. Turn dough out onto a lightly floured surface. Lightly sprinkle flour over top of dough. Using a lightly floured rolling pin, roll dough into a 3/4-inch-thick rectangle (about 9 x 5 inches). Fold dough in half so short ends meet. Repeat rolling and folding process 4 more times.

4. Roll dough to 1/2-inch thickness. Cut with a 2-inch floured round cutter, reshaping scraps and flouring as needed.

5. Place dough rounds on a parchment paper-lined jelly-roll pan. Bake in preheated oven until lightly browned, about 10 minutes. Brush tops with melted butter after removing from the oven. Serve with Sorghum Butter.

Sorghum Butter: Stir together 1 cup (8 oz.) softened butter and 1/2 cup sorghum syrup in a small bowl until blended. Transfer to parchment paper and roll into a log; cover and chill up to 1 month. **Makes about 1 cup**

Speckled Sausage Gravy

MAKES **ABOUT 2 CUPS** ACTIVE **10 MIN.** TOTAL **20 MIN.**

Lots of freshly ground black pepper dots this classic cream gravy for a speckled effect. Serve over biscuits, fried chicken, or pork chops. Serve this in a mini fondue pot on the board to keep it warm and add height to the setup.

8 oz. mild ground pork sausage

1/4 cup (1 1/8 oz.) all-purpose flour

2 1/3 cups whole milk

1/2 tsp. salt

1/2 tsp. black pepper

1/4 tsp. crushed red pepper

2 Tbsp. minced fresh flat-leaf parsley

1. Cook sausage in a large skillet over medium, stirring until it crumbles and is no longer pink. Remove sausage and drain on paper towels, reserving 1 tablespoon drippings in skillet.

2. Whisk flour into hot drippings until smooth; cook, whisking constantly, 1 minute. Gradually whisk in milk, and cook, whisking constantly, 5 to 7 minutes or until thickened. Stir in sausage, salt, black pepper, crushed red pepper, and parsley.

Tater Tot Skewers

SERVES 8 ACTIVE 12 MIN. TOTAL 45 MIN.

Tater tots are a crowd-pleaser, and these skewers are like a loaded baked potato on a stick, making them a perfect, savory addition to any meal of the day. Pile the skewers on the board with the skewer ends facing one direction for easy pickup.

1 (32-oz.) pkg. frozen tater tots

1 (1-oz.) pkg. ranch seasoning

1/2 tsp. salt

16 wooden skewers

4 oz. shredded Monterey Jack cheese (1 cup)

4 oz. shredded cheddar cheese (about 1 cup)

4 slices bacon, cooked and chopped

2 Tbsp. chopped fresh chives

Ketchup (optional)

1. Preheat oven to 425°F. Line a rimmed baking sheet with parchment paper.

2. Combine tater tots, ranch seasoning, and salt in a bowl; toss to coat. Transfer to prepared baking sheet. Bake in preheated oven until golden brown, 20 to 24 minutes. Allow to cool for a few minutes.

3. Thread tots onto 16 (10- to 12-inch) wooden skewers. Return to baking sheet. Top with cheeses and bacon. Bake in preheated oven until cheese is melted, 10 minutes. Remove from oven.

4. Arrange skewers on serving board and sprinkle with chives. Serve with ketchup, if desired.

Slow-Cooker Apple Butter

MAKES 5 CUPS ACTIVE 25 MIN.
TOTAL 10 HOURS, 25 MIN.

Instead of standing for hours at the stovetop, let your slow cooker do the work making this delicious homemade apple butter. Serve this in a bowl with a small knife for slathering. Send your guests home with small jars of apple butter as a parting favor.

5 lb. mixed apples (such as Gala, Granny Smith, Honeycrisp, or Golden Delicious), peeled and cored

3 cups granulated sugar, divided

1 1/2 tsp. ground cinnamon

1/2 tsp. ground nutmeg

1/2 tsp. ground cloves

1. Cut apples into 1-inch cubes; place apple cubes and 1½ cups of the sugar in a 6-quart slow cooker. Cover and cook on HIGH 6 hours.

2. Stir in cinnamon, nutmeg, cloves, and remaining 1½ cups sugar. Cover; cook on LOW until apples are very soft, 4 hours.

3. Place half of apple mixture in a blender. Secure lid on blender, and remove center piece to allow steam to escape. Place a clean towel over opening. Pulse until smooth or to desired texture; repeat with remaining apple mixture. Cool completely. Store in an airtight container in the refrigerator up to 1 month.

The Creole Brunch Board

This board brims with distinctive New Orleans flavor with its mix of simple recipes (some can be made ahead), plus additions to pick up from the grocery store. Offer a few pickled things to prime palates. Heat and slice andouille sausage links to serve with toothpicks. Spoon the Muffuletta dip on crostini, arrange cut-up veggies for dipping, and include a bowl of toasted new-crop pecan halves for nutty crunch.

MAKE

GRITS WAFFLE BITES WITH BACON-PRALINE SYRUP (RECIPE P. 74)

MINI CRUSTLESS QUICHES (RECIPE P. 74)

LAGNIAPPE CHEESE STRAWS (RECIPE P. 75)

MUFFULETTA DIP (RECIPE P. 75)

BUY

ANDOUILLE SAUSAGE (SLICED)

GRAINY MUSTARD

CROSTINI OR MELBA TOAST

CELERY STICKS

CARROT STICKS

PICKLED OKRA

OLIVES

PECAN HALVES (TOASTED)

DRINK

Julia Reed's Bloody Mary: Stir together 6 cups tomato juice, 1¼ cups lime juice, ½ cup Worcestershire sauce, 4 dashes hot sauce, 1 Tbsp. kosher salt, and 1 Tbsp. prepared horseradish. Add cracked black pepper to taste. Refrigerate in an airtight container up to 3 days. To serve, pour 3 Tbsp. vodka in a tall glass filled with ice. Stir in bloody Mary mix. **Makes about 2 quarts mix**

Grits Waffle Bites with Bacon-Praline Syrup

SERVES **8** ACTIVE **25 MIN.** TOTAL **50 MIN.**

Enjoy grits for breakfast in a new way. The rustic texture and not-too-sweet flavor of these waffles make them a lovely backdrop for an array of toppings. Arrange the bite-size waffles on a cutting board or tray with a bowl of warm syrup for dunking or drizzling. These can be made ahead and warmed in the oven. Best of all, they freeze well, too.

½ cup uncooked regular yellow grits	1¼ cups (about 5⅜ oz.) all-purpose flour
6 Tbsp. (3 oz.) cold unsalted butter, cubed	1 Tbsp. granulated sugar
¾ cup whole buttermilk	2 tsp. baking powder
2 large eggs, lightly beaten	½ tsp. baking soda
	Bacon-Praline Syrup (recipe follows)

1. Bring 2 cups water to a boil over medium-high in a medium saucepan. Whisk in grits; return to a boil. Reduce heat to low; cook, stirring often, 15 minutes or until tender. Stir in butter until melted; cool to room temperature. Stir in buttermilk and eggs.

2. Whisk together flour and next 3 ingredients in a small bowl. Stir flour mixture into grits mixture until just combined.

3. Cook batter in a preheated, oiled mini-style waffle iron 3½ to 4 minutes or until golden (about ½ Tbsp. batter per waffle).

Bacon-Praline Syrup

½ cup (4 oz.) butter	2 thick hickory-smoked bacon slices, cooked and crumbled
½ cup chopped pecans	
½ cup pure maple syrup	

Cook butter, pecans, maple syrup, and bacon in a saucepan over medium-low, stirring often, 5 minutes or until blended and sugar dissolves. Serve warm. **Makes about 1 cup**

Mini Crustless Quiches

MAKES **48 (SERVING SIZE: 2 PIECES)**
ACTIVE **20 MIN.** TOTAL **50 MIN.**

These tasty mini quiches are easily made ahead. Freeze half the batch and reheat for breakfast bites on busy mornings. Shredded Swiss, Fontina, or Ggouda are great stand-ins for the cheddar cheese for a change of pace.

6 scallions, thinly sliced	½ tsp. salt
2 Tbsp. chopped fresh flat-leaf parsley	¼ tsp. crushed red pepper
6 large eggs plus 3 large egg yolks	1½ cups whole milk
2 oz. Parmesan cheese, grated (about ½ cup)	2 oz. sharp cheddar cheese, shredded (about ½ cup)

1. Place racks in upper and lower thirds of oven and preheat to 350°F. Coat 2 (24-cup) nonstick mini-muffin pans with cooking spray. Place pans on foil-lined baking sheets. Scatter scallions and parsley over bottom of each cup.

2. Whisk eggs and yolks with Parmesan, salt, and crushed red pepper in a large bowl. Whisk in milk until smooth. Transfer to a cup with a pour spout, and fill each muffin cup with egg mixture. Top each cup with a pinch of cheddar cheese.

3. Bake in preheated oven until quiches are puffed and browned on top, about 30 minutes, rotating pans from top to bottom racks and turning back to front about halfway through.

4. Immediately run a small, sharp knife around outside of each quiche, then invert onto a wire rack to cool. Turn each quiche right side up. Serve warm or at room temperature.

Lagniappe Cheese Straws

MAKES **32 CHEESE STRAWS** ACTIVE **20 MIN.**
TOTAL **50 MIN.**

Lagniappe is a French word that means "a bonus" or "a little something extra." These cheese straws have a lot of extra flavor thanks to Creole seasoning and sharp cheddar. Arrange the straws upright in a glass as you would flowers in a vase to add a bit of height to the food board.

½ (17.3-oz.) pkg. frozen puff pastry sheets, thawed

All-purpose flour for work surface

1 large egg, lightly beaten

3 oz. sharp cheddar cheese, finely shredded (about 1⅓ cups)

1 tsp. Creole seasoning

1. Preheat oven to 400°F. Line 2 baking sheets with parchment paper. Transfer puff pastry sheet to a lightly floured work surface; roll into a 16- x 10-inch rectangle (about ⅛ inch thick). Brush dough lightly with egg; reserve remaining egg. Sprinkle cheese and Creole seasoning over 1 long half of dough rectangle. Fold empty dough half over cheese mixture; press gently. Cut dough crosswise into 32 (5- x ½-inch) strips. Transfer to prepared baking sheets.

2. Working with 1 strip at a time, brush both sides lightly with reserved egg. Twist and gently stretch each strip to about 7 inches long. Bake in preheated oven until golden, 14 to 16 minutes, rotating baking sheets halfway through bake time. Transfer to a wire rack to cool completely, 15 minutes.

Muffuletta Dip

MAKES **ABOUT 4 CUPS** ACTIVE **10 MIN.**
TOTAL **1 HOUR, 10 MIN.**

Make this up to a day before serving to allow the flavors to blend. Parmesan cheese helps hold these ingredients together. You can also serve this versatile recipe with crackers over a block of cream cheese, or toss leftovers in a crunchy iceberg or romaine salad.

1 cup Italian olive salad (such as Boscoli Italian Olive Salad), drained (about 5 oz.)

1 cup diced salami (about 4 oz.)

1 oz. Parmesan cheese, grated (¼ cup)

¼ cup chopped pepperoncini salad peppers

1 (2¼-oz.) can sliced black olives, drained

4 oz. Provolone cheese, diced

1 celery rib, finely chopped

½ red bell pepper, chopped

1 Tbsp. olive oil

¼ cup chopped fresh flat-leaf parsley

Stir together first 9 ingredients. Cover and chill 1 to 24 hours before serving. Stir in parsley just before serving. Serve with crostini or melba toast. Store leftovers in refrigerator up to 5 days.

The Floribbean Sunset Board

Cocktail hour is always festive, but this sundown holiday grazing board takes cues from the flavors you'd find at the southernmost tip of the Sunshine State. Throwing a holiday happy hour is easy with this delicious mix of recipes that you make, rounded out with prepared ingredients that you purchase.

MAKE

WEST INDIES SALAD (RECIPE P. 78)

WAFFLE FRY CUBAN SLIDERS (RECIPE P. 78)

PINEAPPLE SALSA (RECIPE P. 79)

YAM YAKITORI (RECIPE P. 79)

BUY

PLANTAIN CHIPS

GUACAMOLE

KIWIFRUIT (PEEL AND SLICE)

MELON BALLS

CHEESE CUBES

CASHEWS

MACADAMIA NUTS

DRINK

Tropical Champagne Punch: Combine 2 cups pineapple-mango juice, 2 cups orange juice, 2 cups cranberry juice, 2 cups guava nectar, and 1 cup apple juice in a large bowl. Stir in 1 (750-ml) bottle sparkling white wine. **Serves 12**

West Indies Salad

SERVES **6**   ACTIVE **15 MIN.**   TOTAL **15 MIN.**

*Named for the Caribbean islands due south of the tip
of Florida, this salad was the famous staple of Bayley's
Seafood Restaurant in Mobile, Alabama. Bill Bayley Sr. first
whipped it up while at port in the West Indies when he was
serving in the Merchant Marine in the 1940s. The story goes
that he boiled up some spiny Florida lobster, added diced
white onion, and tossed it in an oil-and-vinegar dressing,
and it was a hit. When he opened his restaurant stateside,
he swapped crabmeat for the lobster and the rest is history.
His salad is proof that some of the best things to eat are
often the simplest to make.*

2 lb. fresh jumbo lump
crabmeat, drained and
picked over

²/₃ cup apple cider
vinegar

¹/₂ cup finely chopped
white onion (from 1 small
onion)

¹/₄ cup granulated sugar

¹/₄ cup vegetable oil

2 Tbsp. lemon zest
(from 2 lemons)

2 tsp. kosher salt

1 tsp. black pepper

¹/₄ cup finely chopped
fresh flat-leaf parsley

Small Bibb lettuce leaves
(from 1 head)

Saltine crackers

Place crabmeat, vinegar, onion, sugar, oil, lemon zest, salt,
and pepper in a large bowl, and gently combine. Serve
immediately, or chill, covered, 2 to 3 hours. (Salad is best
after chilling.) Fold in parsley just before serving. Spoon
crab mixture into lettuce leaves, and serve with crackers.

Waffle Fry Cuban Sliders

SERVES **6**   ACTIVE **20 MIN.**   TOTAL **1 HOUR, 5 MIN.**

*While traditional Cuban sandwiches are pressed between
baguette slices and sliders are usually served on mini buns,
these bite-sized wonders are griddled between waffle fries
for a fun and crispy slider spin.*

24 frozen waffle fries

¹/₂ tsp. dry mustard

¹/₂ tsp. garlic salt

Hamburger dill chips,
drained

3 oz. thinly sliced deli
ham

2 oz. sliced Swiss cheese

1 cup baby spinach leaves

1. Preheat oven to 425°F. Toss fries with dry mustard and garlic
salt on a rimmed baking sheet. Bake until crisp and fragrant,
18 to 21 minutes.

2. Divide pickles, ham, cheese, and spinach evenly among
12 waffle fries; top with remaining waffle fries. Lightly coat
sliders with cooking spray.

3. Heat 2 large skillets over medium. Add 6 sliders to one pan;
place second hot skillet on top of sandwiches. Press gently, and
cook 2 minutes on each side or until sandwiches are golden
brown and cheese is melted. Wipe bottom of empty skillet and
reheat. Repeat procedure with remaining sandwiches.

Pineapple Salsa

MAKES 2 CUPS   ACTIVE 15 MIN.   TOTAL 15 MIN.

This juicy tropical salsa is bursting with flavor. It is delicious served simply with plantain chips, but also makes a tasty relish for grilled fish or pork or spooned into shrimp tacos. Make this the morning of the party to knock something off of your recipe to-do list.

1¼ cups chopped fresh pineapple

½ cup chopped red onion (from 1 small onion)

¼ cup chopped fresh cilantro

2 Tbsp. fresh lime juice

1 jalapeño pepper, finely chopped

1 tsp. toasted sesame seeds

1 tsp. pink peppercorns, crushed

Plantain chips

Combine all ingredients in a bowl. Serve with plantain chips.

Yam Yakitori

SERVES 6   ACTIVE 20 MIN.   TOTAL 40 MIN.

Small fingerling sweet potatoes make the perfect bite-size slices. If you can't find them, use regular sweet potatoes and cube them instead.

2½ lb. small fingerling sweet potatoes (about 8 [7- x 1½-in.] potatoes)

½ cup orange juice

½ cup mirin

¼ cup unseasoned rice vinegar

¼ cup soy sauce

2 tsp. packed light brown sugar

12 (8-in.) wooden skewers, soaked in water 30 minutes

1 Tbsp. olive oil

½ tsp. kosher salt

¼ tsp. black pepper

¼ cup thinly sliced scallions (from 2 scallions)

1. Preheat oven to 425°F. Pierce potatoes several times with a fork. Arrange in a single layer in a rimmed baking sheet, and bake just until tender, 25 to 30 minutes. Transfer to a wire rack; cool completely, about 30 minutes.

2. Meanwhile, combine orange juice, mirin, rice vinegar, soy sauce, and brown sugar in a small saucepan over medium, and simmer, stirring often, until thickened, 10 to 15 minutes. Remove from heat; set aside.

3. Peel sweet potatoes, and cut crosswise into 1-inch pieces, discarding ends.

4. Preheat grill to medium (350° to 400°F). Skewer sweet potato pieces. Brush with oil, and sprinkle with salt and pepper; grill, uncovered, 3 minutes. Brush with orange glaze, and continue grilling, turning every 2 to 3 minutes and brushing with glaze after each turn, until charred on both sides. Transfer to a serving platter, and sprinkle with scallions; drizzle evenly with ¾ cup of the orange glaze. Serve immediately with remaining glaze.

The Delta Dessert Board

Dessert parties are always a hit—especially during the holidays. The charcuterie board approach to this downhome spread is a fun way for guests to gather. Arrange ingredients like fresh fruit and nuts artfully among the prepared recipes for lots of wow factor. You can change up the Linzer cookie filling and the types of candy on the board to fit other occasions throughout the year—Easter, Valentine's Day, or Halloween.

MAKE

MISSISSIPPI MUD CAKE SQUARES (RECIPE P. 82)

PEANUT BUTTER-AND-JELLY LINZERS (RECIPE P. 82)

TWICE-SALTED WHITE CHOCOLATE TOFFEE (RECIPE P. 83)

PEPPERMINT PINWHEELS (RECIPE P. 83)

BUY

MARSHMALLOWS

PRALINES

PEPPERMINT CANDY

YOGURT-COVERED PRETZELS

CHOCOLATE KISSES

JORDAN ALMONDS

PISTACHIOS

RASPBERRIES

BLUEBERRIES

DRINK

Eggnog Cocktail: Whisk together 4 cups refrigerated eggnog, ½ cup (4 oz.) bourbon, ¼ cup (2 oz.) coffee liqueur, and 1 tsp. vanilla extract in a pitcher. Serve in coupe glasses rimmed with sparkling sugar. Garnish with a sprinkle of ground cinnamon and nutmeg. **Serves 8**

Mississippi Mud Cake Squares

SERVES 15   ACTIVE 25 MIN.
TOTAL 1 HOUR, 5 MIN., INCLUDING FROSTING

This classic Southern sheet cake is filled with marshmallows and chopped pecans and blanketed in a rich chocolate frosting. Using brownie mix is an easy cheat. Slice the cake into bite-size squares to keep treats on this food board diminutive.

1 cup chopped pecans

2 (6-oz.) pkg. fudge brownie mix (see Note)

1 (10½-oz.) bag miniature marshmallows

Chocolate Frosting (recipe follows)

1. Preheat oven to 350°F. Place pecans in a single layer on a baking sheet. Bake 8 to 10 minutes or until toasted.

2. Prepare mix according to package directions; pour batter into a greased 15- x 10- x 1-inch jelly-roll pan. Bake in preheated oven for 25 minutes. Remove from oven, and top with marshmallows; bake 8 to 10 minutes more.

3. Drizzle warm cake with Chocolate Frosting, and sprinkle evenly with toasted pecans. Cut into bite-size squares.

Note: We used Duncan Hines Chocolate Lover's Double Fudge Brownie Mix.

Chocolate Frosting

½ cup (4 oz.) butter

⅓ cup (about 1 oz.) unsweetened cocoa

⅓ cup milk

1 (16-oz.) pkg. powdered sugar

1 tsp. vanilla extract

Stir together first 3 ingredients in a medium saucepan over medium until butter is melted. Cook, stirring constantly, 2 minutes or until slightly thickened; remove from heat. Beat in powdered sugar and vanilla with an electric mixer on medium-high speed until smooth. **Makes about 2 cups**

Peanut Butter- and-Jelly Linzers

MAKES 18 COOKIES   ACTIVE 40 MIN.
TOTAL 1 HOUR, 30 MIN.

We gave the classic Linzer cookie a PB&J makeover. Use strawberry jam for a pop of red.

1 cup (8 oz.) unsalted butter, softened

½ cup granulated sugar

½ cup packed light brown sugar

½ cup creamy peanut butter

1 large egg yolk

1 tsp. vanilla extract

3 cups (about 12¾ oz.) all-purpose flour

½ tsp. kosher salt

½ tsp. baking powder

½ cup (2 oz.) powdered sugar

½ cup strawberry jam or grape jelly

Banana chips (optional)

1. Preheat oven to 375°F with oven racks in the top third and bottom third of oven. Beat butter, granulated sugar, brown sugar, and peanut butter with an electric mixer on medium speed until smooth, about 1 minute. Add egg yolk and vanilla; beat on low just until incorporated. Whisk together flour, salt, and baking powder. Gradually add to butter mixture, beating on low speed just until incorporated.

2. Place dough on a well-floured surface, and roll to ¼-inch thickness. Cut dough with a 2½-inch round cutter. Gently reroll scraps once, and repeat process with round cutter. Place half of the dough rounds on parchment paper-lined baking sheets. Using a 1½-inch round cutter, cut out and remove dough circles from the center of the remaining half of dough rounds. (Reserve and bake dough round cutouts later, if desired.) Transfer cookies to lined baking sheets.

3. Bake cookies in preheated oven just until set, about 12 minutes. Switch pans top rack to bottom rack halfway through baking. Transfer pans to wire racks to cool cookies completely, about 30 minutes.

4. Sift powdered sugar over cookies with star cutouts. Spread 1½ teaspoons jam on 1 side of remaining cookies. Place a star cutout cookie, powdered sugar-side up, over each jam-covered cookie, and gently press. Stick a banana chip into grape jelly centers, if desired.

Twice-Salted White Chocolate Toffee

SERVES 18 (SERVING SIZE: 2 PIECES)
ACTIVE 15 MIN. TOTAL 1 HOUR, 25 MIN.

This sinful treat can be made well ahead of time, but be warned—it might be tempting to gobble it up before the party. Saltine crackers add crunch and a lightly salted base, while sea salt on top tempers the sweetness of this cracker candy.

1 cup (8 oz.) salted butter, plus more to grease pan

54 saltine crackers (about 1½ sleeves)

1 cup packed dark brown sugar

1 (12-oz.) pkg. white chocolate chips

1 cup chopped toasted pecans

¼ tsp. Maldon sea salt (optional)

1. Preheat oven to 350°F. Line an 18- x 12-inch rimmed baking sheet with aluminum foil. Grease foil with butter. Arrange crackers in prepared pan to fit and completely cover bottom.

2. Bring the 1 cup butter and brown sugar to a boil in a heavy saucepan over medium, whisking occasionally. Boil, whisking constantly, 3 minutes. Carefully pour mixture over crackers; spread evenly.

3. Bake in preheated oven until bubbly all over, 8 to 10 minutes. Carefully transfer baking sheet from oven to a wire rack. Let stand 1 minute. Sprinkle white chocolate chips over top; let stand until chips soften, about 2 minutes. Spread white chocolate over brown sugar mixture. Sprinkle with pecans and, if desired, sea salt. Let stand at room temperature 30 minutes. Chill toffee until firm, about 30 minutes. Store in an airtight container up to 1 week in refrigerator.

Peppermint Pinwheels

MAKES ABOUT 5 DOZEN ACTIVE 30 MIN.
TOTAL 4 HOURS

Kids love these swirly cookies with a hint of mint. Swap out the red food coloring for green, if you prefer.

1 cup (8 oz.) salted butter, softened

1½ cups granulated sugar

1 large egg

1 tsp. peppermint extract

1 tsp. vanilla extract

2½ cups (about 10⅝ oz.) all-purpose flour

1½ tsp. baking powder

¼ tsp. table salt

Red food coloring paste or gel

1. Beat butter with a heavy-duty stand mixer on medium speed until creamy, about 2 minutes; gradually add sugar, beating well. Add egg and extracts, beating until combined.

2. Stir together flour, baking powder, and salt in a small bowl. Gradually add to butter mixture, beating on low speed just until blended.

3. Divide dough in half; add desired amount of red food coloring to 1 portion, and knead until color is distributed. Shape dough halves into disks; wrap in plastic wrap, and chill until firm, about 1 hour.

4. Divide each dough disk into 2 equal portions. Roll out each portion on floured wax paper into an 8-inch square, trimming edges if necessary.

5. Invert 1 white dough square onto 1 red dough square; peel wax paper from white dough. Tightly roll up dough, jelly-roll fashion, peeling paper from red dough as you roll. Repeat with remaining dough squares. Wrap rolls in plastic wrap, and chill 2 hours.

6. Preheat oven to 350°F. Remove dough from refrigerator; cut into ¼-inch-thick slice, and place slices 2 inches apart on parchment paper-lined baking sheets.

7. Bake in preheated oven in batches until bottoms are lightly browned, 10 to 12 minutes. Transfer cookies from pans to wire racks, and cool completely.

Game Night

One-dish casual dinners make cooking and cleanup a cinch, which is welcome during this season of hosting and toasting. These hearty skillet, sheet pan, and slow-cooker recipes are Test Kitchen-approved and ideal for enjoying with family and friends while playing games by the fire.

Smoked Fish Hash

½ cup sour cream

½ cup full-fat Greek yogurt

2 Tbsp. prepared horseradish

½ tsp. Worcestershire sauce

½ tsp. white wine vinegar

4 Tbsp. butter

2 medium (6 oz. each) unpeeled russet potatoes, boiled, cooled, and diced

1 small red onion, finely chopped

1 Granny Smith apple, diced

Kosher salt and freshly ground black pepper

Pinch of cayenne pepper

½ cup heavy cream

1 (4-oz.) smoked trout fillet, flaked into ½-inch pieces

1 tsp. thinly sliced fresh chives

½ tsp. minced fresh rosemary

Lemon wedges

Equally at home on your stove or over a campfire, this fragrant skillet meal can also be served for breakfast. Try substituting sweet potatoes for russets. Other smoked fish, such as bluefish or whitefish, can be used in place of the smoked trout. Or, use thinly sliced smoked salmon, cut it into pieces, and drape it over the hash just before serving to gently warm through.

1. Heat a 12-inch cast-iron skillet over medium-high 5 minutes. Stir together sour cream and next 4 ingredients in a small bowl, and chill until ready to use.

2. Melt butter in skillet over medium-high heat; add potatoes, and cook, turning occasionally, about 10 minutes or until potatoes begin to brown and crisp. Add onion and apple, and cook, stirring occasionally, about 10 minutes or until onion is tender and apple is golden.

3. Add salt and black pepper to taste; add cayenne pepper. Stir in cream. Cook, without stirring, until potatoes are deep golden, about 5 minutes. Using a metal spatula, gently lift and turn hash. Cook 5 minutes; gently stir in trout and herbs. Remove from heat, and squeeze lemon wedges over hash. Serve immediately with sour cream sauce.

ADD A SIMPLE SIDE
Butter Lettuce Toss

Serve butter lettuce leaves tossed with your fruitiest extra-virgin olive oil and a splash of champagne vinegar. Season simply with salt and freshly ground black pepper.

King Ranch Chicken Cheesy Mac

SERVES **6**   ACTIVE **20 MIN.**   TOTAL **45 MIN.**

King Ranch casserole and mac-and-cheese collide in this one-pan comfort food classic that's a win for game night. What's not to love?

½ (16-oz.) pkg. cavatappi pasta

2 Tbsp. butter

1 medium yellow onion, diced

1 red bell pepper, diced

1 (10-oz.) can diced tomatoes and green chiles

1 (8-oz.) pkg. pasteurized prepared cheese product, cubed

3 cups chopped cooked chicken

1 (10¾-oz.) can condensed nacho cheese soup (such as Campbell's Fiesta Nacho Cheese Soup)

½ cup sour cream

½ cup chopped fresh cilantro

1 tsp. taco seasoning

1½ cups shredded 4-cheese Mexican blend (6 oz.)

1. Preheat oven to 350°F. Prepare pasta according to package directions.

2. Meanwhile, melt butter in a large Dutch oven over medium-high heat. Add onion and bell pepper, and sauté 5 minutes or until tender. Stir in tomatoes and green chiles and prepared cheese product; cook, stirring constantly, 2 minutes or until cheese melts. Stir in chicken, next 5 ingredients, and hot cooked pasta until blended. Lightly grease a 10-inch cast-iron skillet or an 11- x 7-inch baking dish with cooking spray. Spoon mixture into skillet; sprinkle with shredder cheese. Bake in preheated oven until bubbly, 25 to 30 minutes.

ADD A SIMPLE SIDE

Lemony Broccolini

Steam broccolini in microwave or on the stovetop until crisp-tender. Toss with olive oil, salt, freshly ground black pepper, and the finely grated zest of 1 lemon. Serve with lemon wedges.

Cast-Iron Commandments

These tips help cast-iron pans last forever.

1. **Use Often:** The more you use it, the better it will work.

2. **Clean After Use:** Wash the pan with hot water while it's still warm.

3. **Avoid Soap:** (Except for No. 9 below). Never put it in the dishwasher.

4. **Scour Smartly:** Use coarse salt for scouring. Rub salt around the pan with a paper towel. Still sticking? Loosen residue by boiling water in the pan and scraping with a spatula.

5. **Dry Thoroughly:** Heat over low heat 2 minutes after rinsing to open the pores of the iron. Use a paper towel and tongs to coat pan with a light film of vegetable oil.

6. **Store in a Cool, Dry Place:** For pans with lids, add a paper towel wad, and keep ajar to let air flow.

7. **Seasoning 411:** Seasoning is the polymerization of fat bonded to the pan's surface. It creates a glossy sheen that makes cast-iron nonstick and protects it from rust. Maintaining it is key to cast-iron care.

8. **Bust the Rust:** Rub out rust on cast iron with steel wool. For stubborn rust, take the cast iron to a machine shop to have it sand-blasted. Then start the seasoning process (below) to build up a protective coat.

9. **Season It:** Here's the best way to season a neglected skillet.
Wash Vigorously: After busting the rust, wash—just this once—with warm soapy water; dry.
Rub with Vegetable Oil: Rub oil inside, outside, and on skillet handle. Wipe away excess.
Bake at 400°F for 1 Hour: Place the pan upside-down, on oven rack; line bottom rack with foil. Bake. Repeat oiling and baking until seasoned.

10. **Pass It Down:** Well-seasoned pans get better with age. Be sure to leave this lasting heirloom in your will.

Pork Chops with Roots and Greens

SERVES **4**   ACTIVE **10 MIN.**   TOTAL **40 MIN.**

Roasted pork chops and beets combine with hearty kale in this colorful winter salad tossed with a tangy thyme-honey mustard dressing. Whip up the dressing in Step 3 up to a day in advance.

1 lb. mixed yellow, red, and orange baby beets, peeled and halved

2 tsp. minced garlic (about 3 garlic cloves)

3 Tbsp. olive oil, divided

1 tsp. kosher salt, divided

¾ tsp. black pepper, divided

4 (12-oz.) bone-in pork loin chops

¼ cup sour cream

1 Tbsp. Dijon mustard

1 Tbsp. honey

1 Tbsp. chopped fresh thyme, divided

3 cups finely shredded curly kale (stems removed)

1. Preheat broiler with oven rack about 10 inches from heat. Toss together beets, grated garlic, 1 tablespoon of the oil, and ¼ teaspoon each of the salt and pepper. Place on a large, lightly greased, aluminum foil-lined rimmed baking sheet. Broil 10 minutes.

2. Meanwhile, rub pork chops with 1 tablespoon of the olive oil, and sprinkle with ½ teaspoon of the salt and ¼ teaspoon of the pepper. Remove beets from oven, and nestle pork chops into beets. Return pan to oven. Bake until pork is just cooked through and beets are tender, about 15 minutes.

3. Whisk together sour cream, mustard, honey, 1 teaspoon of the thyme, ¼ teaspoon each of the salt and pepper, and remaining 1 tablespoon oil in a small bowl. Transfer beets to a large bowl, and add shredded kale and 2 tablespoons of the dressing; toss to coat. Cover with plastic wrap; let stand 5 minutes. Serve pork chops over vegetables. Sprinkle with remaining 2 teaspoons thyme and remaining dressing.

Sheet Pan Cleanup

Lining a sheet pan with parchment paper or foil protects it from baked-on spills and greasy messes. Spraying it with cooking spray is another worthy option that works with some recipes. Even with steadfast pan prep, sheet pans do require TLC from time to time. Here's our Test Kitchen's favorite method:

Sprinkle a generous amount of baking soda on the pan, cover it in hydrogen peroxide, and sprinkle another layer of baking soda on top. Let stand for up to 2 hours (the longer it soaks, the more residue comes off). Wipe the pan with a sponge to reveal a grime-free surface that looks almost as good as new—no heavy scrubbing required.

ADD A SIMPLE SIDE

Cheesy Cornbread

Top purchased or prepared cornbread with shredded cheddar, and broil until cheese is melted and bubbly. Slice and serve warm.

Mini Meatloaves with Winter Vegetables

A medley of ground beef and vegetables gets topped with a tangy soy-ketchup glaze in these mini meatloaves that bake up tender and delicious alongside roasted red potatoes, Brussels sprouts, and leeks. Prepare the meatloaf mixture a day ahead, and store it, covered, in the refrigerator until you're ready to form the meatloaves before baking.

5 Tbsp. olive oil

2 tsp. chopped garlic (about 2 garlic cloves)

1 tsp. tangerine zest, plus 2 Tbsp. fresh juice (from 1 tangerine)

1 tsp. kosher salt, divided

¾ tsp. black pepper, divided

12 oz. Brussels sprouts, halved

1 leek, chopped (about 1½ cups)

8 oz. red potatoes, cut into wedges

8 oz. lean ground beef

8 oz. mild ground pork sausage

¼ cup grated carrot (from 1 carrot)

¼ cup grated yellow onion (from 1 onion)

¼ cup dry breadcrumbs

1 large egg, lightly beaten

2 Tbsp. tomato paste

1 Tbsp. honey

2 tsp. unseasoned rice vinegar

Pinch ground cloves

1 tsp. soy sauce

1 Tbsp. thinly sliced fresh chives

1. Preheat oven to 400°F. Whisk together oil, garlic, tangerine zest, juice, ½ teaspoon of the salt, and ¼ teaspoon of the pepper in a large bowl. Add Brussels sprouts, leek, and red potatoes, and toss to coat. Spread the vegetables on a lightly greased, aluminum foil–lined rimmed baking sheet. Bake vegetables for 10 minutes.

2. Meanwhile, combine beef, sausage, carrot, onion, breadcrumbs, egg, and remaining ½ teaspoon each salt and pepper in a large bowl. Mix gently just until combined. Shape into 4 (2- x 3-inch) loaves. Remove pan from oven, push vegetables to 1 side, and carefully place meatloaves on pan. Return pan to oven, and bake until meat is cooked through and vegetables are tender, about 35 minutes.

3. Mix together tomato paste and next 4 ingredients in a small bowl. Spread over meatloaves. Increase oven temperature to broil, and broil until sauce begins to brown, about 2 minutes. Divide meatloaves and vegetables evenly among 4 plates. Sprinkle with chives.

ADD A SIMPLE SIDE
Quick Kale Salad

Drizzle 3 Tbsp. olive oil over 5 oz. baby kale leaves. Season with salt and black pepper. Massage leaves; set aside for 5 minutes. Toss with the juice of 1 lemon and ⅓ cup shaved Parmesan cheese.

Slow-Cooker Brisket Chili

SERVES 8   ACTIVE 30 MIN.   TOTAL 9 HOURS

3 Tbsp. (about 1 oz.) all-purpose flour

2 Tbsp. ancho chile powder

1 Tbsp. ground cumin

1 Tbsp. kosher salt

1 tsp. dried oregano

2 1/2 lb. beef brisket, trimmed and cut into 1-inch cubes

4 Tbsp. olive oil, divided

1 (14 1/2-oz.) can fire-roasted diced tomatoes, drained

1 (4 1/2-oz.) can chopped green chiles, undrained

1 orange bell pepper, chopped

1 medium-size red onion, chopped (about 1 cup)

2 large garlic cloves, minced (about 1 Tbsp.)

3/4 cup beef broth

1 Tbsp. fresh lime juice (from 1 lime)

Cilantro-Lime Crema (recipe follows)

Corn chips

What's the best part of this recipe? Set it and forget it. A flavor-packed ingredients list that includes a healthy dose of spices, lots of veggies, and a zesty crema drizzle (plus the quick prep time) takes this chili to the next level.

1. Stir together first 5 ingredients in a small bowl. Toss spice mixture with brisket cubes until well coated.

2. Heat 2 tablespoons of the oil in a large skillet over medium-high. Add half of brisket cubes, and cook, stirring often, until browned on all sides, 5 to 7 minutes. Transfer to a 6-quart slow cooker. Repeat procedure with remaining oil and brisket.

3. Stir tomatoes, green chiles, bell pepper, onion, garlic, and beef broth into slow cooker. Cover and cook on LOW until beef is tender, about 8 hours. Uncover and cook until slightly thickened, about 30 minutes. Stir in lime juice. Serve with Cilantro-Lime Crema and corn chips.

Cilantro-Lime Crema: Stir together 1/2 cup sour cream; 1/4 cup chopped fresh cilantro; 2 Tbsp. mayonnaise; 1 tsp. lime zest, plus 1 Tbsp. fresh juice (from 1 lime); and 1/4 tsp. kosher salt in a medium bowl. Cover and chill at least 15 minutes or until ready to serve. Refrigerate in an airtight container up to 2 days. **Makes about 3/4 cup**

Slow-Cooker Warming Drawer

You probably already love your slow cooker for the convenience of hands-off cooking it provides, but we think you'll love it even more when you learn how it can warm bowls and plates when you're entertaining a crowd. Thirty minutes before your meal is ready to be served, stack 6 to 8 bowls or 10 to 12 plates in the bottom of a large slow cooker lined with a damp kitchen towel. Set the heat to LOW and cover until the meal is ready. The bowls or plates will be warm, but not too hot to handle.

ADD A SIMPLE SIDE

Ranch Slaw

Toss 2 bags of shredded coleslaw mix with 1/2 cup ranch dressing and a small (3 1/2-oz.) jar of capers—juice and all. Season with freshly ground black pepper, sliced scallions, chopped fresh cilantro, and the finely grated zest and juice of 2 lemons. Let sit 10 minutes before serving.

Christmas Day Buffet

A bountiful buffet is a festive way to showcase a beautiful holiday spread, like this menu for eight, without crowding the dining table with platters and dishes. Kick off the meal with the salad course, then arrange the main attractions on the sideboard and let guests return to fill their dinner plates.

AVOCADO, GRAPEFRUIT, AND BUTTER LETTUCES

HONEY YEAST ROLLS   **PROSCIUTTO-WRAPPED TURKEY ROULADE**

GREEN BEANS WITH CANDIED PECANS AND MAPLE VINAIGRETTE

WILD RICE DRESSING   HASSELBACK POTATO CASSEROLE

CHOCOLATY PEPPERMINT CHEESECAKE

Avocado, Grapefruit, and Butter Lettuces

SERVES 8   ACTIVE 15 MIN.   TOTAL 15 MIN.

Avocado lends creaminess to this salad of cool-season gems. Substitute other varieties of grapefruit or citrus like blood oranges, tangerines, or pomelos.

2 large Ruby Red grapefruit	2 tsp. chopped fresh chervil
1 Tbsp., plus 1 tsp. Dijon mustard	¼ cup walnut oil
1 tsp. kosher salt	2 large heads butter or Boston lettuce
½ tsp. black pepper	4 avocados, cut into wedges
2 tsp. chopped fresh oregano	¼ cup chopped toasted walnuts

1. Finely grate 1 grapefruit to yield 2 teaspoons zest; set aside.

2. Slice off stem end and base of each grapefruit, exposing pulp inside. Place 1 grapefruit on a cutting board with flat base down. Cut off a 2-inch-wide strip of peel and white pith, slicing deeply along the curved side to expose pulp inside. Cut another strip from opposite side of fruit, and continue, alternating sides, completely exposing fruit. Discard peel and pith. Repeat with remaining grapefruit.

3. Working over a bowl to catch juice and fruit, remove grapefruit segments from pith using a small, sharp knife. Hold fruit in 1 hand and a small, sharp knife in the other, slicing along inside wall of 1 segment from outside to center. Slice other side to release segment into bowl. Continue around the fruit, squeezing core over bowl to capture all the juice. Repeat with remaining grapefruit.

4. Combine zest, mustard, salt, pepper, oregano, and chervil in a separate large bowl. Whisk in ¼ cup of the grapefruit juice, followed by the oil. Gently toss half the lettuce leaves in dressing, and arrange in the bottom of a salad bowl.

5. Toss half the avocado slices carefully in remaining dressing; arrange on top of lettuce in bowl. Top with half the grapefruit segments. Repeat. Sprinkle top of salad with walnuts.

Honey Yeast Rolls

MAKES 2 DOZEN   ACTIVE 17 MIN.
TOTAL 2 HOURS, 17 MIN.

Try your hand at homemade rolls this year. A heavy-duty stand mixer makes quick work of these dinner plate delicacies. This recipe makes a big batch, so you have extra rolls for tomorrow's turkey roulade sandwiches.

2 cups warm whole milk (100°F to 110°F)	¼ cup honey
2 (¼-oz.) envelopes active dry yeast	2½ tsp. kosher salt
2 tsp. granulated sugar	½ cup (1 stick), plus 2 Tbsp. melted butter, divided
6 cups (about 25½ oz.) all-purpose flour	2 large eggs, lightly beaten

1. Stir together first 3 ingredients in a 1-quart glass measuring cup; let stand 5 minutes.

2. Combine flour, honey, and salt in the bowl of a heavy-duty electric stand mixer. Add 6 tablespoons melted butter, the eggs, and yeast mixture; beat on low speed, using dough-hook attachment, 3 minutes or until blended and a soft dough forms. Increase speed to medium-low, and beat 4 minutes or until dough is smooth and elastic but still slightly sticky. Cover bowl of dough with plastic wrap, and let rise in a warm (85°F) place, free from drafts, 1 hour or until doubled in bulk.

3. Lightly grease two 13- x 9-inch pans with cooking spray. Punch dough down. Turn dough out onto a lightly floured surface. Divide dough into 24 equal portions. Gently shape each portion into a 2-inch ball; place in prepared pans. Brush tops with 2 tablespoons melted butter. Cover and let rise in a warm (85°F) place, free from drafts, 45 minutes or until doubled in bulk.

4. Preheat oven to 375°F. Bake rolls until golden brown, 15 minutes. Transfer rolls from pan to a wire rack, and brush with remaining 2 tablespoons melted butter. Serve warm, or cool completely.

Prosciutto-Wrapped Turkey Roulade

SERVES 8   ACTIVE 1 HOUR, 10 MIN.
TOTAL 1 HOUR, 45 MIN.

Save yourself time and have your butcher debone and butterfly the turkey breast for you. The cranberry-port sauce takes this roast to the next level.

8 thick-cut bacon slices, chopped	20 prosciutto slices
2 shallots, minced	6 (6-inch) fresh rosemary sprigs
4 garlic cloves, minced	½ cup dried unsweetened cranberries
¼ tsp. crushed red pepper	1 cup port
2 (20-oz.) pkg. fresh baby spinach	½ cup red wine vinegar
Kosher salt and black pepper	1 cup chicken broth
	2 Tbsp. plum jam
1 bone-in, skin-on turkey breast (6- to 7-lb. total)	1 Tbsp. cold butter

1. Cook bacon in a Dutch oven over medium 10 to 15 minutes or until crisp. Remove bacon, and drain on paper towels, reserving 3 tablespoons drippings in Dutch oven. Cook shallots, garlic, and crushed red pepper in hot drippings 1 to 2 minutes or until tender. Add spinach, in batches, and cook 5 minutes or until wilted. Remove mixture; coarsely chop. Stir together bacon and spinach mixture in a large bowl; add salt and black pepper to taste. Cool 10 minutes.

2. Remove bone from turkey. Butterfly turkey breasts by making a lengthwise cut in 1 side, cutting to but not through the opposite side; unfold. Place breasts between 2 sheets of heavy-duty plastic wrap, and flatten to ¼-inch thickness, using a rolling pin or the flat side of a meat mallet. Sprinkle both sides with desired amount of salt and black pepper.

3. Arrange 10 of the prosciutto slices on a work surface in a slightly overlapping fashion. Place turkey breast, skin-side down, on top of prosciutto slices. Spoon half of spinach mixture on 1 breast, leaving a ½-inch border. Roll up prosciutto and turkey breast, jelly-roll fashion, starting with long skinless side. Place 3 rosemary sprigs on top of prosciutto-wrapped breast, and tie with kitchen string, securing at 2-inch intervals.

Repeat procedure with remaining prosciutto, breast, spinach mixture, and rosemary sprigs.

4. Line a baking sheet with aluminum foil and place in oven. Preheat oven to 350°F. Bring cranberries and port to a boil in a medium saucepan over high. Reduce heat to medium-low; simmer, stirring occasionally, 5 minutes or until cranberries are tender. Remove from heat.

5. Transfer breasts to prepared baking sheet in oven. Bake in preheated oven until a meat thermometer inserted into thickest portion registers 165°F, 45 minutes to 1 hour.

6. Transfer turkey to a wire rack. Discard fat in Dutch oven. Add cranberry mixture and vinegar to Dutch oven, and cook over medium-high heat, stirring constantly, 4 to 5 minutes or until thickened. Stir in broth, and simmer, stirring occasionally, 5 to 8 minutes or until reduced by half. Stir in plum jam, and cook, stirring constantly, 1 minute. Whisk in butter and salt and pepper to taste.

7. Remove and discard kitchen string from turkey. Cut turkey into thin slices, and serve with cranberry mixture.

Green Beans with Candied Pecans and Maple Vinaigrette

SERVES 8   ACTIVE 15 MIN.   TOTAL 20 MIN.

Maple syrup adds distinctive sweetness to the vinaigrettethat clings to the quick-cooked beans topped with nutty pecans for a simple side that rival green bean casserole.

¾ cup pecans	¼ cup packed dark brown sugar
Kosher salt and black pepper	¼ cup olive oil
2 lb. green beans, trimmed	2 Tbsp. red wine vinegar
¼ cup, plus 1 Tbsp. (2½ oz.) butter	2 Tbsp. Dijon mustard
3 shallots, finely chopped	1 Tbsp. pure maple syrup

1. Preheat oven to 350°F. Spread pecans on a rimmed baking sheet and bake, tossing once, until toasted, 6 to 8 minutes. Let cool, then roughly chop.

2. Bring a large pot of water to a boil and add 2 teaspoons salt. Add green beans and cook until just tender, 4 to 5 minutes. Drain and run under cold water to cool.

3. Melt butter in a small skillet over medium. Add shallots and cook until soft and translucent, about 3 minutes. Add sugar and pecans, and stir until sugar melts and pecans are coated, about 1 minute. Remove from heat.

4. Whisk together oil, vinegar, mustard, maple syrup, ½ teaspoon salt, and ¼ teaspoon pepper in a large bowl. Add green beans and pecans; toss to combine. Serve warm or at room temperature.

Wild Rice Dressing

SERVES 10   ACTIVE 15 MIN.   TOTAL 40 MIN.

Wild rice, pistachios, apples, and pomegranate arils combine in a dressing full of flavor and crunch.

5 sourdough bread slices, cut into ½-inch cubes

2 Tbsp. unsalted butter, melted

2 Tbsp. extra-virgin olive oil

1 cup chopped celery (about 3 stalks)

1 medium-size red onion, diced (about 1 cup)

2 Honeycrisp or Pink Lady apples, diced

4 cups cooked wild rice

1 cup shelled salted pistachios, roughly chopped

2 Tbsp. chopped fresh flat-leaf parsley

1 Tbsp. chopped fresh rosemary

1 Tbsp. fresh lemon juice

2 tsp. kosher salt

½ tsp. black pepper

½ cup pomegranate arils

¼ cup firmly packed fresh flat-leaf parsley leaves

1. Preheat oven to 400°F. Toss bread cubes with melted butter in a medium bowl. Spread on a baking sheet, and bake until crispy and lightly browned, 5 to 8 minutes.

2. Heat oil in a skillet over medium-high. Add celery and onion, and cook, stirring occasionally, until tender, about 8 minutes.

Add apples; cook, stirring, until apples are tender-crisp and browned, 5 to 7 minutes. Stir in toasted bread cubes, the rice, pistachios, chopped parsley, rosemary, lemon juice, salt, and pepper. Cook until heated through, about 3 minutes. Spoon onto a serving platter. Garnish with pomegranate arils and parsley leaves.

Hasselback Potato Casserole

SERVES 12   ACTIVE 30 MIN.   TOTAL 1 HOUR, 45 MIN.

Hasselback potatoes get their name from the Swedish Potato à la Hasselbacken. The flavorful infused cream settles into the potato slices while they bake.

3½ lb. russet potatoes, peeled (about 4 medium)

2 cups heavy cream

¼ tsp. grated nutmeg

⅛ tsp. black pepper

1½ tsp. kosher salt, divided

½ cup dry breadcrumbs

1 oz. Parmesan cheese, grated (about ¼ cup)

3 Tbsp. unsalted butter, melted

3 Tbsp. chopped fresh oregano

1. Cut potatoes into ⅛-inch-thick slices, using a mandoline or a knife. Bring a large pot of water to a boil over high. Add slices; cook until just softened, 3 minutes. Drain. Spread in a single layer on a paper towel-lined baking sheet. Set aside until cool and dry, about 20 minutes. Arrange slices, standing vertically on edges, in a greased 13- x 9-inch broiler-proof baking dish.

2. Bring cream to a simmer in a saucepan over medium. Whisk in nutmeg, pepper, and 1 teaspoon salt. Cook, stirring, until thickened slightly, about 10 minutes. Pour over potatoes. Cover and chill until ready to bake, up to 1 day ahead.

3. Stir together breadcrumbs cheese, butter, and remaining ½ teaspoon salt in a small bowl. Stir in oregano, and set aside.

4. Preheat oven to 350°F. Remove casserole from refrigerator. Bake, covered, 45 minutes. Uncover and top evenly with crumb mixture. Return to oven, and bake 15 minutes. Increase oven temperature to broil, and broil until topping is golden brown, about 5 minutes. Let stand 10 minutes before serving.

Chocolaty Peppermint Cheesecake

SERVES 10 TO 12   ACTIVE 30 MIN.
TOTAL 11 HOURS, 50 MIN.

A rich, dark crust and a snowy white chocolate filling combine in this peppermint-spiked cheesecake. Don't worry if your cheesecake cracks; the light and fluffy layer of whipped cream will cover any flaws.

CRUST

2 cups chocolate wafer crumbs (about 35 wafers)

5 Tbsp. (2½ oz.) butter, melted

3 Tbsp. granulated sugar

FILLING

1 cup white chocolate baking chips (such as Ghiradelli)

¼ cup heavy cream

4 (8-oz.) pkg. cream cheese, softened at room temperature

1 cup granulated sugar

1 tsp. vanilla extract

1 tsp. peppermint extract

4 large eggs

ADDITIONAL INGREDIENTS

Whipped Peppermint Cream (recipe follows)

Crushed peppermint candies or candy canes, crumbled peppermint bark, for garnish

1. Prepare Crust: Preheat oven to 350°F. Stir together first 3 ingredients in a medium bowl. Press mixture on bottom and 1 inch up sides of a lightly greased (with cooking spray) 9-inch springform pan. Bake 10 minutes. Let stand at room temperature until ready to use.

2. Prepare Filling: Reduce oven temperature to 325°F. Microwave baking chips and cream in a small microwave-safe bowl on MEDIUM (50% power) 1 to 1½ minutes or until melted and smooth, stirring every 30 seconds. Cool 10 minutes.

3. Beat cream cheese and sugar with a heavy-duty electric stand mixer on medium-low speed just until smooth. Add white baking chip mixture and extracts, and beat on low speed just until blended. Add eggs, 1 at a time, beating on low speed just until yellow disappears after each addition; pour into prepared crust.

4. Bake at 325°F until center of cheesecake jiggles and is almost set, 50 minutes to 1 hour. Remove cheesecake from oven, and gently run a knife around outer edge of cheesecake to loosen from sides of pan. (Do not remove sides.) Cool cheesecake completely on a wire rack (about 2 hours). Cover and chill 8 hours or up to 2 days.

5. Remove sides of pan. Spread Whipped Peppermint Cream over cheesecake, and top with crushed peppermint candies or crumbled bark.

Whipped Peppermint Cream: In a large bowl, beat 2 cups heavy cream and ¾ tsp. peppermint extract with a mixer on medium-high speed until foamy; gradually add ¾ cup powdered sugar, beating until soft peaks form. **Make about 4 cups**

Morning Glories

Whether you have little ones pleading to see Santa's surprises at the break of day, or you simply want to coax late-risers downstairs to start unwrapping the gifts beneath the tree, this menu entices with bright colors, bold flavors, and something to suit the sweet tooth, health nut, and hearty appetite found in every household.

RED BERRY COFFEE CAKE CITRUS MOSAIC SALAD
CHEDDAR-AND-LEEK STRATA **RED-EYE SLUSHIES**

Red Berry Coffee Cake

SERVES 10   ACTIVE 20 MIN.   TOTAL 1 HOUR

This coffee cake is delicious served warm or at room temperature and can be made with any frozen red berry you fancy—raspberries, strawberries, cranberries, or even cherries.

1 large egg

½ cup whole milk

½ cup plain yogurt

3 Tbsp. vegetable oil

2 cups (8½ oz), plus 1 Tbsp. all-purpose flour

½ cup granulated sugar

4 tsp. baking powder

¾ tsp. kosher salt

1½ cups frozen blueberries

2 Tbsp. turbinado sugar

2 Tbsp. sliced almonds

¼ tsp. ground cinnamon

1. Preheat oven to 400°F. Whisk together first 4 ingredients in a large bowl.

2. Sift together 2 cups flour and next 3 ingredients in another bowl. Stir flour mixture into egg mixture just until dry ingredients are moistened.

3. Toss 1¼ cups blueberries in remaining 1 tablespoon flour; fold into batter. Pour into a lightly greased 9-inch springform pan. Sprinkle with remaining ¼ cup blueberries.

4. Stir together turbinado sugar, sliced almonds, and cinnamon; sprinkle over batter.

5. Bake in preheated oven until a wooden pick inserted in center comes out clean, 25 to 30 minutes. Cool in pan on a wire rack 15 minutes; remove sides of pan.

Citrus Mosaic Salad

SERVES 8   ACTIVE 20 MIN.   TOTAL 1 HOUR, 20 MIN.

This beautiful fruit salad is a perfect match for this menu. Its tart, juicy flavors temper the richness of the egg strata and the sweetness of the coffee cake. Using a medley of citrus fruit simply makes this a visual stunner, but you can use whatever citrus you prefer here.

1 medium blood orange, peeled and cut into ¼-inch rounds

2 medium tangerines, peeled and cut into ¼-inch rounds

1 medium Ruby Red or Rio Star grapefruit, peeled and cut into ¼-inch rounds

1 medium Oro Blanco or Marsh grapefruit, peeled and cut into ¼-inch rounds

½ cup pomegranate arils

¼ cup toasted pine nuts

2 Tbsp. powdered sugar, optional

Small fresh mint leaves

Arrange fruit in a mosaic pattern on a large platter. Top with pomegranate arils and pine nuts. Sift powdered sugar over fruit, if desired. Garnish with mint.

Cheddar-and-Leek Strata

SERVES 8 TO 10   ACTIVE 35 MIN.
TOTAL 10 HOURS, 10 MIN.

Breakfast casseroles like this one are ideal for entertaining holiday guests. This can be assembled up to 24 hours before baking. Just be sure to set aside an hour for it to come to room temperature before you pop it in the oven to bake into rich, custardy perfection.

1/2 (16-oz.) Italian bread loaf, cubed (about 5 cups)

6 Tbsp. (3 oz.) butter, divided

2 cups shredded cheddar cheese(8 oz.)

2 oz. Parmesan cheese, grated (1/2 cup)

1 leek, trimmed and thinly sliced (about 1 cup)

1 tsp. minced garlic

3 Tbsp. all-purpose flour

11/2 cups chicken broth

3/4 cup dry white wine

1/2 tsp. salt

1/2 tsp. freshly ground pepper

1/4 tsp. ground nutmeg

1/2 cup sour cream

Kosher and black salt

8 large eggs, lightly beaten

1/4 cup chopped fresh flat-leaf parsley

Chopped fresh chives

1. Place bread cubes in a well-buttered 13- x 9-inch baking dish. Melt 3 tablespoons butter, and drizzle over bread cubes. Sprinkle with cheeses.

2. Melt remaining 3 tablespoons butter in a medium saucepan over medium; add leek and garlic. Sauté 3 to 5 minutes or until tender. Whisk in flour until smooth; cook, whisking constantly, 2 to 3 minutes or until lightly browned. Whisk in broth and next 4 ingredients until blended. Bring mixture to a boil; reduce heat to medium-low, and simmer, stirring occasionally, 15 minutes or until thickened. Remove from heat. Stir in sour cream. Add salt and black pepper to taste.

3. Gradually whisk about one-fourth of hot sour cream mixture into eggs; add egg mixture to remaining sour cream mixture, whisking constantly. Whisk in parsley, and pour mixture over cheese and bread in baking dish. Cover with plastic wrap, and chill 8 to 24 hours.

4. Let strata stand at room temperature 1 hour. Preheat oven to 350°F. Remove plastic wrap, and bake 30 minutes or until set. Sprinkle with chives.

Red-Eye Slushies

SERVES 8   ACTIVE 10 MIN.   TOTAL 10 MIN.

Spiked or not, this bright slushie is an eye-opening morning pick-me-up. Keep a small pitcher of simple syrup nearby for those who like their slurps sweeter.

1/2 cup fresh lime juice (from 4 limes)

1/2 cup fresh lemon juice (from 3 lemons)

1/2 cup simple syrup

1 cup frozen orange juice concentrate, thawed (from 1 [12-oz.] container)

1 cup frozen cranberry juice concentrate, thawed (from 1 [12-oz.] container)

6 cups ice cubes

Vodka (optional)

Ginger ale

Luxardo cherries

Orange slices

Process lime juice, lemon juice, simple syrup, orange juice concentrate, cranberry juice concentrate, and ice cubes in a blender on high until mixture is smooth and slushy, 30 to 45 seconds. Divide slushy evenly among 8 glasses. Stir 1½ ounces vodka into each, if desired. Top each glass with 1 to 2 ounces ginger ale. Garnish with cherries and orange slices.

Savor & Share

A HOLIDAY COOKBOOK

Go Dutch!

Turn to the workhorse pot of every kitchen—the Dutch oven—to brown, braise, and simmer up flavorful feasts with the fringe benefit of a one-pan cleanup. Including succulent lemon chicken, savory Mediterranean-style turkey legs, beautiful holiday ham, crusty lamb shanks, and ginger tea-infused short ribs, these recipes take you from Thanksgiving right into the New Year.

ONE-POT LEMON CHICKEN   BRAISED TURKEY LEGS WITH FRUIT, OLIVES, AND ALMONDS   BOURBON-GLAZED HAM WITH ORANGES PECORINO-CRUSTED LAMB SHANKS WITH GREEN SAUCE SPIKED GINGER-TEA SHORT RIBS WITH CILANTRO GREMOLATA

One-Pot Lemon Chicken

1 tsp. black pepper

2 tsp. kosher salt, divided

6 bone-in, skin-on chicken breasts

3 Tbsp. olive oil

¼ cup granulated sugar

3 lemons, halved

1 orange, quartered

1 cup pitted dates or prunes

3 garlic cloves, crushed

1 large onion, chopped

1 cinnamon stick

¾ cup dry white wine

3 bay leaves

6 fresh thyme sprigs

1 cup chicken broth

2 Tbsp. butter

Bright, bold flavors meld deliciously in this chicken dish. Bone-in breasts are meaty and cook perfectly in the moist heat of the braise.

1. Preheat oven to 325°F. Sprinkle pepper and 1½ teaspoons salt evenly over chicken. Cook 3 chicken breasts, skin-side down, in 1½ tablespoons hot oil in a large Dutch oven over medium 4 minutes or until skin is golden brown and crisp. Remove chicken from Dutch oven; wipe Dutch oven clean with paper towels. Repeat procedure with remaining 1½ tablespoons oil and 3 chicken breasts; reserve 2 tablespoons drippings in Dutch oven.

2. Sprinkle sugar over cut sides of lemon halves and orange quarters. Cook fruit, cut sides down, in hot drippings in Dutch oven over medium-high until fruit browns and sugar melts and begins to bubble, about 5 minutes. Reduce heat to medium-low, and cook 3 minutes. Add dates and next 3 ingredients; cook, stirring often, 3 minutes more.

3. Increase heat to high, and stir in wine. Bring mixture to a simmer, stirring to loosen browned bits from bottom of Dutch oven. Cook 3 to 5 minutes or until almost all liquid has evaporated. Stir in bay leaves, thyme, and broth. Nestle chicken in date mixture. Place a piece of parchment paper directly on chicken, and cover Dutch oven with a tight-fitting lid.

4. Bake in preheated oven or until chicken is tender, 1 hour and 30 minutes. Let chicken stand, covered, in Dutch oven at room temperature 30 minutes. Discard parchment paper. Transfer chicken to a platter; cover to keep warm.

5. Skim any fat from surface of cooking liquid. Pour cooking liquid through a fine wire-mesh strainer into a saucepan. Reserve lemons and oranges; discard remaining solids. Bring sauce to a simmer over medium-hight. Remove from heat; add butter and whisk until sauce is smooth. Garnish chicken with lemons and oranges, and serve with sauce.

General Oven-to-Slow Cooker Conversion Guide

OVEN COOK TIME	SLOW COOKER (LOW)	SLOW COOKER (HIGH)
15 to 30 min.	4 to 5 hours	2 to 3 hours
30 to 45 min.	6 to 8 hours	3 to 4 hours
45 min. to 3 hours	8 to 10 hours	4 to 6 hours

Note: Dishes that cook in the oven at 350°F or lower are the best options for converting to the slow cooker. If an oven recipe doesn't call for liquid, add ½ cup liquid with the food being cooked. If the oven recipe calls for liquid, reduce the amount by half for the slow cooker.

Braised Turkey Legs with Fruit, Olives, and Almonds

SERVES 6   ACTIVE 1 HOUR, 20 MIN.
TOTAL 15 HOURS, 50 MIN.

Don't be put off by the timing here. Seasoning the legs and putting them in the fridge uncovered overnight allows them to soak up lots of flavor while air-drying to crisp up the skin, which is key for browning in the pan before braising.

6 fresh turkey legs (about 5 lb.)

3/4 tsp. kosher salt

1/2 tsp. freshly ground black pepper

1 tsp. ground ginger

1 tsp. ground cumin

1 tsp. ground coriander

1/2 tsp. ground turmeric

1/8 tsp. cayenne pepper

2 Tbsp. olive oil

8 large shallots, peeled and sliced

1 1/2 cups chicken broth

1 tsp. Meyer lemon zest

1/4 cup fresh Meyer lemon juice

12 pitted prunes, chopped

1/2 cup halved pitted Castelvetrano olives

4 cups hot cooked couscous

1/2 cup toasted Marcona almonds, lightly chopped

1/4 cup chopped fresh oregano

Lemon wedges

1. Season turkey legs with salt, black pepper, and next 5 ingredients. Rub mixture all over turkey legs to coat. Place turkey legs in a single layer on a rack in a jelly-roll pan; chill, uncovered, 12 to 24 hours.

2. Preheat oven to 350°F. Let turkey stand at room temperature 30 minutes. Cook 3 turkey legs in hot oil in Dutch oven over medium-high 10 minutes until well browned on all sides. Remove the turkey legs from the pan and set aside. Repeat with remaining turkey legs.

3. Cook shallots in drippings over medium 5 minutes, stirring constantly, or until tender. Add broth, stirring to loosen any browned bits from bottom of skillet. Stir in Meyer lemon zest and juice. Return turkey legs to the pan, and add the prunes and olives. Place a piece of parchment paper directly on turkey leg,s and cover the pot with a tight-fitting lid.

4. Bake in preheated oven until meat pulls away from bone, 1 1/2 to 2 hours. Remove from heat, and let turkey stand in Dutch oven, covered with parchment and lid, at room temperature 30 minutes. Discard parchment paper.

5. Preheat broiler with oven rack 7 inches from heat. Carefully remove turkey legs from Dutch oven and place on a lightly greased rack in a broiler pan.

6. Broil turkey 2 to 3 minutes or until skin is crisp and golden brown. Cover loosely with aluminum foil. Pour liquid from Dutch oven through a strainer into a glass measuring cup; let stand 5 minutes. Skim fat from the surface; discard fat.

7. Serve turkey legs over couscous. Sprinkle with almonds and oregano. Serve with lemon wedges and sauce.

Bourbon-Glazed Ham with Oranges

1 (13- to 14-lb.) fully cooked bone-in ham

½ cup (4 oz.) bourbon

2 cups orange preserves

⅔ cup packed dark brown sugar

4 navel oranges (or 6 to 8 clementines), peeled and thinly sliced

A layer of citrus slices looks like a lacquered mosaic when the ham is removed from the oven. If you don't have a hinged V-rack insert that works in your Dutch oven, a rack can be improvised by lining the bottom of the pot with metal cookie cutters. For an edible rack, use a layer of root vegetables like carrots or potatoes to lift the ham off the bottom of the pot while it cooks. Recipes call for fully cooked hams to be heated to 140°F because it is the optimum temperature for bringing out the most flavor.

1. Preheat oven to 350°F. Line a Dutch oven with aluminum foil. Lightly grease a large hinged V-rack; place on top of the foil. Score ham on all sides and place fat-side up on rack.

2. Stir together bourbon, preserves, and brown sugar in a bowl. Brush ham with 1 cup of the bourbon glaze. Arrange the orange (or clementine) slices on top of the ham, overlapping slightly. Brush with a bit of remaining glaze. Roast in the preheated oven for 1 hour, brushing with bourbon glaze after 30 minutes.

3. Remove ham from oven. Increase oven temperature to 400°F. Baste ham with additional bourbon glaze. Return to oven for 15 minutes. Remove from oven; brush with more glaze. Return to oven until a thermometer inserted in thickest portion of ham registers 140°F, 10 to 15 minutes. Remove from oven; rest 10 minutes. Slice and serve warm or at room temperature with any remaining bourbon glaze.

Bone Up on Ham

Bone-in ham: This ham has the entire bone intact. It's available whole, butt end, or shank end only.

Boneless ham: This ham has the entire bone removed, and the ham is rolled or packed in a casing.

Country ham: This ham is prepared with a dry-rub cure. Most country hams are very dry and salty, and require soaking before cooking. They're often named for the city in which they're processed. Smithfield ham, from Smithfield, Virginia, is one of the most popular types of country-cured ham.

Dry-cured ham: The surface of this ham is rubbed with a mixture of salt, sugar, nitrites, and seasonings, and then air-dried.

Fresh ham: This is an uncured, uncooked hind leg of the pig.

Smoked ham: This ham is hung in a smokehouse after the curing process to take on the smoky flavor of the wood used.

Pecorino-Crusted Lamb Shanks with Green Sauce

SERVES **6**   ACTIVE **1 HOUR**   TOTAL **5 HOURS**

Pecorino-Romano is an aged, dry, crumbly cheese that's less expensive than Parmigiano-Reggiano, plus it's easy to grate, making it ideal for creating the beautiful and flavorful crust on these luscious shanks. Get a jump start by preparing the recipe through Step 3; cover and chill. Skim any solid fat off the top, reheat shanks and sauce, and pick back up with Step 4.

6 lamb shanks

Kosher salt and black pepper

1/4 cup olive oil

2 Tbsp. tomato paste

1 cup red wine

1 (10 1/2-oz.) can beef consommé

6 fresh flat-leaf parsley sprigs

4 fresh thyme sprigs

4 bay leaves

3 (1-inch) lemon peel strips

2 celery ribs, cut into 1-inch pieces

1 large carrot, cut into 1-inch pieces

1 onion, cut into wedges

1 fresh rosemary sprig

4 Tbsp. butter, divided

1 1/2 cups panko (Japanese breadcrumbs)

1 cup finely grated fresh Pecorino-Romano cheese

2 1/2 tsp. chopped fresh thyme, plus sprigs for garnish

1 tsp. chopped fresh rosemary, plus sprigs for garnish

Green Sauce (recipe follows)

1. Preheat oven to 325°F. Season lamb with salt and black pepper; let stand at room temperature 30 minutes. Cook 3 shanks in 2 tablespoons hot oil in a large Dutch oven over medium-high 2 minutes on each side. Remove shanks, and repeat procedure with remaining shanks and oil, reserving drippings in Dutch oven.

2. Cook tomato paste in drippings about 30 seconds or until tomato paste chars slightly. Add wine; bring to a boil, stirring to loosen browned bits from pan. Boil 3 minutes or until mixture is reduced to 1/3 cup. Stir in consommé, next 8 ingredients, and 1 cup water. Return shanks to Dutch oven. Place parchment paper directly on shanks; cover with a tight-fitting lid.

3. Bake in preheated oven until meat is very tender and pulls away from bones, about 3 hours. Let shanks stand, covered with parchment and lid, in Dutch oven at room temperature 30 minutes.

4. Melt 2 tablespoons butter in a skillet over medium-high; add panko, and cook, stirring often, 1 minute or until lightly browned. Toss panko mixture with cheese, and chopped thyme and rosemary. Place mixture in a shallow bowl.

5. Preheat broiler with oven rack 7 inches from heat. Discard parchment paper from lamb shanks. Remove shanks from Dutch oven. Dredge each shank in panko mixture, pressing to adhere. Spray shanks lightly with cooking spray, and place on a lightly greased rack in a broiler pan. Broil 2 to 3 minutes on each side, or until coating is golden and crisp. Transfer shanks to a platter, garnish with thyme and rosemary sprigs; cover loosely to keep warm while making the Green Sauce.

6. Serve shanks with Green Sauce on the side.

Green Sauce

2 cups loosely packed fresh flat-leaf parsley leaves

3/4 cup loosely packed fresh mint leaves

2 Tbsp. chopped fresh rosemary

2 Tbsp. white wine vinegar

1 garlic clove, grated

1 tsp. finely grated lemon zest

1 cup olive oil

1 tsp. kosher salt

1 tsp. crushed red pepper

Process parsley, mint, rosemary, vinegar, garlic, and lemon zest in a food processor 20 seconds. With machine running, pour oil into mixture until blended, 20 seconds. Stir in salt and crushed red pepper. **Makes about 1 1/2 cups**

Spiked Ginger-Tea Short Ribs with Cilantro Gremolata

SERVES 4   ACTIVE 45 MIN.   TOTAL 8 HOURS

These short ribs get dressed with bright sauce and verdant herb topping that is a spin on the classic gremolata you find served with braised dishes like osso bucco. Serve the short ribs atop grits, mashed potatoes, or egg noodles.

3 lb. bone-in beef short ribs, trimmed

1 tsp. black pepper

3 tsp. kosher salt, divided

2 Tbsp. canola oil

5 cups sliced red onions (from 3 medium)

8 garlic cloves, minced (about 3 Tbsp.)

2 (3-inch) pieces fresh ginger, sliced

1 cup (8 oz.), plus 1½ Tbsp. (³⁄₄ oz.) rye whiskey, divided

1½ cups sweet tea

1½ cups beef broth

2 Tbsp. sherry vinegar

2 Tbsp. cornstarch

2 Tbsp. warm water

½ cup chopped fresh cilantro

½ cup chopped scallions (about 4 scallions)

3 Tbsp. orange zest

3 tsp. fresh orange juice

2 tsp. extra-virgin olive oil

1. Preheat oven to 325°F. Sprinkle short ribs with pepper and 2 teaspoons of the salt. Heat canola oil in a Dutch oven over medium-high. Add ribs, and cook until well browned, about 15 minutes, turning once.

2. Add onions, garlic, ginger, and ½ teaspoon of the salt to skillet, and cook over medium-high, stirring often, until onions are very tender, 8 to 10 minutes. Add 1 cup of the whiskey, and cook 1 minute. Stir in tea and broth, and bring to a simmer, about 3 minutes. Pour onion mixture over ribs in Dutch oven. Bake, covered, in the preheated oven until meat is very tender and falling off the bone, 2½ to 3 hours.

3. Remove ribs, and set aside. Pour mixture from Dutch oven through a fine-mesh strainer into a medium saucepan; discard solids. Cook liquid in pan over medium-high until reduced by half, 10 to 12 minutes. Add sherry vinegar, ¼ teaspoon of the salt, and remaining 1½ tablespoons whiskey. Stir together cornstarch and warm water; stir into mixture in pan, and bring to a simmer, 2 to 3 minutes. Remove from heat.

4. Combine cilantro, scallions, orange zest, orange juice, olive oil, and remaining ¼ teaspoon salt in a small bowl. Serve ribs with sauce, and top with gremolata.

Side Ways

Holiday dinners can never have too many side dishes. Whether you offer a beautiful self-serve spread on a sideboard or kitchen island or pass platters family-style at the table, these colorful and delicious seasonal favorites from our Test Kitchen might just steal the spotlight from the main course.

KALEIDOSCOPE SALAD   APPLE-PECAN WILD RICE DRESSING

NEW SCHOOL GREEN BEAN CASSEROLE   **BLOOMING SWEET POTATOES**

OYSTER CASSEROLE

Kaleidoscope Salad

SERVES 8 TO 10   ACTIVE 20 MIN.   TOTAL 20 MIN.

Perfect for a sideboard, the warm vinaigrette softens these sturdy greens, but their structure holds up well for an hour or two. Prep all the ingredients well ahead of time, and refrigerate until you are ready to toss with the vinaigrette. Try Chioggia beets with their candy-stripe interiors here.

8 oz. thick applewood-smoked bacon slices, coarsely chopped

1 cup sliced yellow onion

1½ tsp. kosher salt, divided

¾ tsp. freshly ground black pepper, divided

½ cup white wine vinegar

2 Tbsp. maple syrup

1 bunch Lacinato kale, stemmed and coarsely chopped (about 7 cups)

1 bunch rainbow Swiss chard, stemmed and coarsely chopped (about 8 cups)

1 small red beet, thinly sliced

1 small yellow or orange beet, thinly sliced

½ cup toasted pumpkin seeds

½ cup dried cherries

½ cup crumbled feta cheese

1. Cook bacon in a large skillet over medium, stirring occasionally, 6 to 8 minutes or until crisp; remove bacon using a slotted spoon, and drain on paper towels. Reserve 6 tablespoons drippings in skillet. Add onion, ½ teaspoon salt, and ¼ teaspoon pepper, and cook 2 minutes. Remove from heat.

2. Add white wine vinegar to skillet, and stir to loosen browned bits from bottom of skillet. Whisk in maple syrup.

3. Toss together chopped kale, Swiss chard, onion mixture, and remaining 1 teaspoon salt and ½ teaspoon pepper in a large bowl. Transfer to a serving platter. Top with cooked bacon, beet slices, pumpkin seeds, dried cherries, and feta cheese.

Apple-Pecan Wild Rice Dressing

SERVES 10   ACTIVE 15 MIN.   TOTAL 40 MIN.

Wild rice, apples, and walnuts combine to make a dressing full of flavor and crunch.

5 sourdough or Italian bread loaf slices, cut into ½-inch cubes (about 3 cups)

2 Tbsp. unsalted butter, melted

2 Tbsp. extra-virgin olive oil

1 cup chopped celery (about 3 stalks)

1 medium-size red onion, diced

2 Honeycrisp or Sweet Tango apples, diced

4 cups cooked wild rice

1 cup toasted pecans, roughly chopped

2 Tbsp. chopped fresh flat-leaf parsley

1 Tbsp. minced fresh rosemary

1 Tbsp. fresh orange juice

2 tsp. kosher salt

½ tsp. black pepper

¼ cup firmly packed fresh flat-leaf parsley leaves

1. Preheat oven to 400°F. Toss bread cubes with melted butter in a medium bowl. Spread on a baking sheet, and bake until crispy and lightly browned, 5 to 8 minutes.

2. Heat oil in a skillet over medium-high. Add celery and onion; cook, stirring occasionally, until tender, about 8 minutes. Add apples; cook, stirring occasionally, until apples are tender-crisp and browned, 5 to 7 minutes. Stir in toasted bread cubes, rice, pecans, chopped parsley, rosemary, orange juice, salt, and pepper. Cook until heated through, about 3 minutes. Spoon onto a serving platter. Top with parsley leaves.

New School Green Bean Casserole

SERVES **10** ACTIVE **1 HOUR, 15 MIN.**

TOTAL **2 HOURS**

3 lb. green beans, trimmed and halved crosswise

2 Tbsp. olive oil

3 cups sliced fresh mushrooms

1 cup chopped red onion (from 1 large onion)

1 Tbsp. minced garlic (about 3 garlic cloves)

¼ cup dry white wine

¼ cup all-purpose flour

2 cups whole milk

½ (8-oz.) pkg. cream cheese, softened

1½ tsp. kosher salt

½ tsp. black pepper

⅛ tsp. freshly ground nutmeg

1 (8-oz.) can diced water chestnuts, drained

2 medium leeks (about 1½ lb.)

1 cup canola oil

1. Bring a large pot of water to a boil over high. Add green beans; return to a boil, and cook 2 minutes. Drain green beans, and rinse under cold running water to cool. Spread in a single layer on paper towels to drain. Let stand at room temperature until completely dry, about 45 minutes.

2. Meanwhile, heat olive oil in a large skillet. Add mushrooms and onion, and cook, stirring often, until softened, about 8 minutes. Add garlic and wine, and cook until most of the wine evaporates, about 2 minutes. Sprinkle flour over mushroom mixture, and cook, stirring constantly, 1 minute. Add milk, and bring to a simmer, stirring constantly. Cook, stirring constantly, until thickened, about 2 minutes. Stir in cream cheese, salt, pepper, and nutmeg until smooth.

3. Transfer green beans to a lightly greased 13- x 9-inch baking dish, and toss with water chestnuts. Pour milk mixture evenly over green beans, and stir to coat. Spread in an even layer; cover with aluminum foil. Chill until ready to bake.

4. Preheat oven to 350°F. Remove casserole from refrigerator while oven preheats. Bake, covered, until hot and bubbly around the edges, about 1 hour.

5. While beans bake, cut leeks in half lengthwise; cut each half into 2- to 3-inch pieces. Thinly slice into long strips (about 2 cups thin strips). Heat canola oil in a small saucepan over medium-high to 350°F. Fry leeks in hot oil, in 2 to 3 batches, until golden, 1 to 2 minutes per batch. Remove with a slotted spoon, and drain on paper towels. Sprinkle fried leeks over hot casserole just before serving.

Blooming Sweet Potatoes

SERVES **8** ACTIVE **10 MIN.** TOTAL **50 MIN.**

3 large sweet potatoes (2½ to 3 lb.), peeled and cut into ¼-inch-thick slices

4½ Tbsp. olive oil, divided

2½ tsp. kosher salt, divided

1 tsp. black pepper, divided

3 center-cut bacon slices

½ cup diced yellow onion

1 Tbsp. chopped fresh thyme

4 tsp. pure maple syrup, divided

1. Preheat oven to 475°F. Toss together sweet potato slices with 2½ tablespoons olive oil, ½ teaspoon salt, and ½ teaspoon pepper. Spread in a single layer in a jelly-roll pan. Bake just until tender, turning once, about 10 minutes. Cool on wire racks 10 minutes. Transfer to a bowl. Reduce oven temperature to 425°F.

2. Heat a 10-inch cast-iron skillet over medium. Cook bacon 5 minutes. Increase heat to medium-high, and cook until golden brown. Remove bacon, reserving drippings in skillet. Crumble bacon. Reduce heat to medium; add onion to skillet, and cook until translucent, about 2 minutes. Stir in remaining 2 tablespoons oil, the thyme, remaining 2 teaspoons salt, remaining ½ teaspoon pepper, and 2 teaspoons of the maple syrup. Add mixture to sweet potato slices; toss to combine.

3. Starting at the outer edge of the same skillet, arrange sweet potato slices in slightly overlapping concentric circles to form a flower shape. Bake at 425°F until sweet potatoes are tender and edges begin to crisp, about 40 minutes. Drizzle with remaining 2 teaspoons maple syrup. Top with bacon.

Oyster Casserole

8 Tbsp. cold butter, divided, plus more for greasing dish

1½ tsp. kosher salt

1 tsp. black pepper

¼ tsp. dried thyme

⅛ tsp. ground nutmeg

2 pt. fresh shucked oysters, undrained

1 cup heavy cream or whipping cream

One (9-oz.) pkg. oyster crackers (such as Premium Soup & Oyster Crackers), divided

1 Tbsp. chopped fresh flat-leaf parsley

Top this with homemade breadcrumbs instead of oyster crackers if you wish.

1. Generously butter a 13- x 9-inch baking dish. Preheat oven to 350°F. Cut 6 tablespoons of the butter into ½-inch pieces, and set aside. Stir together salt, pepper, thyme, and nutmeg in a small bowl, and set aside.

2. Pour oysters in liquid over a fine-mesh strainer into a medium bowl. Measure ⅓ cup strained oyster liquid into a small bowl. (Discard remaining oyster liquid, or reserve for another use.) Stir cream into oyster liquid. Cut any large oysters into 2 or 3 pieces. Microwave remaining 2 tablespoons butter in a medium-size microwavable glass bowl on HIGH until melted, about 30 seconds. Crush 1 cup of the oyster crackers and add to butter. Stir to coat, and set aside.

3. Sprinkle bottom of prepared baking dish with one-fourth of the remaining crackers. Arrange one-fourth of the oysters, spaced a few inches apart, over crackers. Sprinkle with one-fourth of the seasoning mixture. Arrange one-fourth of the butter pieces around the oysters. Repeat layers 3 times using remaining oyster crackers, oysters, seasoning mixture, and butter pieces. Sprinkle evenly with reserved melted butter-cracker mixture.

4. Pour oyster liquid-cream mixture over layered mixture in baking dish. Bake in preheated oven until puffed up, firm, and heated through, 30 to 35 minutes. Sprinkle with parsley. Serve hot or warm.

Pie for the Course

Savory or sweet, pies are irresistible treats. Tiny two-bite mushroom-and-cheese pies are a crowd-pleasing cocktail hour snack. Classic skillet pot pie with a golden puff pastry top is a dramatic dinnertime presentation. Sweet red raspberries and tart cranberries accent pies both big and small for a touch of holiday flair and flavor for dessert.

MINI MUSHROOM-AND-GRUYÈRE POT PIES   FLAKY SKILLET POT PIE
MINI RASPBERRY PIES   CHRISTMAS BERRY BUTTERMILK PIE

Mini Mushroom– and–Gruyère Pot Pies

2 Tbsp. unsalted butter

1 Tbsp. olive oil

1 large shallot, finely chopped

8 oz. cremini mushrooms, chopped

2 garlic cloves, minced

1 tsp. chopped fresh chives

1/2 tsp. chopped fresh thyme

1/3 cup dry white wine

2 oz. cream cheese, at room temperature

1/2 cup (2 oz.) shredded Gruyère cheese

1/4 tsp. kosher salt

1/8 tsp. black pepper

1 (14.1-oz.) pkg. refrigerated piecrusts

1 large egg, lightly beaten

Flaky sea salt

Fresh thyme leaves

MAKES **12** ACTIVE **25 MIN.** TOTAL **55 MIN.**

This pretty appetizer recipe calls for leaving every other cup in the muffin pans empty to allow room to crimp the dough edges. These wow tast ebuds whether served warm or at room temperature.

1. Preheat oven to 350°F. Melt butter with olive oil in a large skillet over medium–high. Add shallot; cook, stirring often, until slightly transparent and fragrant, 1 minute. Add mushrooms; cook, stirring occasionally, until mushrooms are tender and lightly browned, about 8 minutes. Add garlic, chives, and chopped thyme; cook, stirring often, until fragrant, 1 minute. Add wine, and cook until liquid is nearly evaporated, 2 minutes more. Remove from heat; let cool slightly, 10 minutes. Mix in cream cheese, shredded Gruyère, kosher salt, and pepper.

2. Coat 2 (12–cup) miniature muffin pans or 1 (24–cup) miniature muffin pan with cooking spray. Unroll both piecrusts on a work surface. Using a 3¼-inch round cutter, cut out 12 dough rounds; using a 2½-inch round cutter, cut out 12 more dough rounds, combining and rolling out remaining dough once, if necessary.

3. Whisk together egg and 1 tablespoon water in a small bowl. Fit a 3¼-inch dough round into every other muffin cup in pans, leaving a small edge at top. Brush edges with some of the egg mixture. Spoon about 1 tablespoon mushroom mixture into each dough cup. Top each filled cup with a 2½-inch dough round, crimping edges of bottom and top crusts together to seal.

4. Brush tops of pies with remaining egg mixture, and sprinkle with flaky sea salt and thyme leaves. Bake in preheated oven until golden brown, 25 to 30 minutes. Cool 5 minutes before serving.

Flaky Skillet Pot Pie

SERVES **6**   ACTIVE **20 MIN.**   TOTAL **1 HOUR, 10 MIN.**

½ cup butter

2 cups thinly sliced leek (from 1 large leek)

1 cup chopped carrots (from 3 medium carrots)

½ cup all-purpose flour, plus more for work surface

2 cups lower-sodium chicken broth

4 cups shredded rotisserie chicken

1 cup frozen petite sweet peas, thawed

½ cup heavy cream

2 tsp. finely chopped fresh thyme

1½ tsp. kosher salt

½ tsp. black pepper

1 large egg

½ (17.3-oz.) pkg. frozen puff pastry sheets, thawed

Everyone will love this classic dish reinvented in a skillet with its buttery freeform crust. To save time, shred the chicken and chop the carrots and leek up to two days ahead. Cover and store in the refrigerator.

1. Preheat oven to 400°F with rack in lower third of oven. Melt butter in a deep 10-inch ovenproof skillet over medium-high. Add leek and carrots. Cook, stirring often, until softened, about 6 minutes. Sprinkle with flour; cook, stirring constantly, 1 minute. Stir in broth; let mixture come to a simmer. Simmer, stirring constantly, until mixture thickens, 1 to 2 minutes. Stir in shredded chicken, peas, cream, thyme, salt, and pepper. Remove from heat; let cool 10 minutes.

2. Whisk together egg and 1 tablespoon water in a small bowl. Roll pastry sheet into a 12-inch square on a lightly floured surface. Cut into 16 (3-inch) squares. Arrange squares on top of chicken mixture in skillet, brushing each square with egg mixture and slightly overlapping squares to cover surface of chicken mixture. Place skillet on a rimmed baking sheet.

3. Transfer baking sheet with skillet to oven, and bake in preheated oven until top is browned and filling is bubbly, about 30 minutes. Let stand 10 minutes before serving.

Mini Raspberry Pies

We used Wilton's nonstick six-cavity Mini Pie Pan. Chill reserved crust rounds while the first batch bakes, and allow the pan to cool completely before beginning the second batch.

PASTRY CRUSTS
¼ cup powdered sugar

2 (14.1-oz.) pkg. refrigerated piecrusts

CREAMY LEMON FILLING
1½ (8-oz.) pkg. cream cheese, softened

1 Tbsp. sour cream

½ cup granulated sugar

2 tsp. lemon zest

1 Tbsp. fresh lemon juice

RASPBERRY TOPPING
5 pints fresh raspberries, divided

1 cup granulated sugar

2 Tbsp. cornstarch

1 Tbsp. butter

VANILLA CREAM
1 cup heavy cream

¼ tsp. vanilla extract

3 Tbsp. powdered sugar

1. Prepare Pastry Crust: Preheat oven to 425°F. Sprinkle work surface with 1 tablespoon powdered sugar. Roll 1 piecrust into a 12½-inch circle on surface, and cut into 3 (6-inch) rounds. Repeat with remaining 3 tablespoons powdered sugar and 3 piecrusts to make 12 rounds. Fit 6 rounds, sugar-side down, into each mold of a 6-cavity mini pie pan; fold edges under, and crimp. Prick bottom and sides with a fork. Chill remaining 6 rounds.

2. Bake in preheated oven until golden brown, about 8 minutes. Cool on a wire rack 5 minutes. Remove crusts from pan to wire rack, and cool completely. Cool pan completely. Repeat procedure with remaining 6 piecrust rounds.

3. Prepare Creamy Lemon Filling: Beat cream cheese and sour cream with an electric mixer on medium speed until smooth. Add ½ cup sugar and lemon zest and juice; beat until smooth and fluffy. Spread about 2½ Tbsp. filling into each cooled piecrust; cover with plastic wrap, and chill until ready to serve (up to 24 hours).

4. Prepare Raspberry Topping: Process 1 pint raspberries in a blender or food processor until smooth; press through a fine-mesh strainer into a 3-quart saucepan, using back of a spoon to squeeze out juice; discard pulp. Stir sugar into juice in pan.

5. Whisk together cornstarch and ¼ cup water; gradually whisk cornstarch mixture into raspberry mixture. Bring to a boil over medium, and cook, whisking constantly, 1 minute. Remove from heat, and whisk in butter. Cool 15 minutes.

6. Toss together raspberry mixture and remaining fresh raspberries gently in a large bowl until coated. Cover; chill 3 hours or until cold.

7. Prepare Vanilla Cream: Beat heavy cream and vanilla on medium-high speed until foamy; gradually add powdered sugar, beating until soft peaks form.

8. Spoon about ½ cup Raspberry Topping into each pie; top with Vanilla Cream. Serve immediately.

DESSERT

Christmas Berry Buttermilk Pie

SERVES **8**   ACTIVE **40 MIN.**   TOTAL **3 HOURS, 35 MIN.,** INCLUDING CRUST

You can use a refrigerated piecrust here, but a food processor makes easy work of from-scratch crust.

1½ cups granulated sugar

3 Tbsp. all-purpose flour

3 large eggs

1 cup buttermilk

½ cup butter, melted

1 Tbsp. loosely packed lemon zest

3 Tbsp. fresh lemon juice

1 tsp. vanilla extract

Perfect Pastry Crust (recipe follows)

2 cups fresh cranberries (thawed if frozen)

Fresh berries, whipped cream, and/or fresh mint, for garnish (optional)

1. Preheat oven to 350°F. Whisk together sugar and flour in a large bowl. Whisk eggs and next 5 ingredients into flour mixture; pour into Perfect Pastry Crust. Sprinkle the cranberries evenly over surface of filling.

2. Bake in preheated oven 35 to 45 minutes or until almost set, covering edges with aluminum foil after 15 minutes. Transfer to a wire rack, and cool 1 hour. Garnish servings with fresh berries, whipped cream, and/or fresh mint, if desired.

Perfect Pastry Crust

1½ cups all-purpose flour

1 Tbsp. granulated sugar

½ tsp. table salt

6 Tbsp. cold butter, cubed

3 Tbsp. cold shortening, cubed

4 to 5 Tbsp. ice water

Parchment paper

1. Pulse first 3 ingredients in a food processor 3 or 4 times or until combined. Add butter and shortening, and pulse 8 to 10 times or until mixture resembles coarse meal. Drizzle 4 Tbsp. ice water over mixture; pulse 4 or 5 times or until dough clumps together, adding up to 1 tablespoon ice water, 1 teaspoon at a time, if necessary. Gently shape dough into a flat disk. Wrap in plastic wrap, and chill 30 minutes.

2. Preheat oven to 400°F. Roll dough into a 12-inch circle (about ⅛ inch thick) on a floured surface. Fit into a 9-inch pie plate; crimp edges. Prick bottom and sides with a fork. Line pastry with parchment paper, and fill with pie weights or dried beans.

3. Bake in preheated oven 10 minutes. Remove weights and parchment paper, and bake 8 to 10 more minutes or until lightly browned. Transfer to a wire rack, and cool completely (about 30 minutes). **Makes 1 (9-inch) crust**

Note: For a sparkly crust, whisk 1 large egg yolk with 1 Tbsp. heavy cream, and brush the crimped edge, lattice top, or top crust, depending on your recipe, and then sprinkle with sanding sugar. Cover edge and top crust with foil if it begins to brown while baking.

Take the Cake

Win hearts and influence people with these irresistible layered, frosted, and glazed confections. Make one to finish your feast, bake one to take to a holiday gathering, or box one up and tie it with a bow for the sweetest gift around. Any way you slice them, these decadent desserts will leave a lasting impression.

GREEN AND RED VELVET SWIRL BUNDT CAKE   LEMON-COCONUT CAKE
ORANGE-ROSEMARY CHEESECAKE   FUDGE CAKE WITH
CARAMEL-BOURBON BUTTERCREAM   GINGERBREAD LATTE CAKE
WITH VANILLA WHIPPED CREAM FROSTING

Green and Red Velvet Swirl Bundt Cake

SERVES 10 TO 12   ACTIVE 30 MIN.

TOTAL 2 HOURS, 45 MIN., INCLUDING GLAZE

The trick to creating looping swirls is to gently layer the batter around the Bundt pan with a small cookie scoop. No need to swirl with a knife—it will marble as it bakes.

1½ cups butter, softened

2½ cups granulated sugar

6 large eggs

3¾ cups all-purpose flour

1 tsp. baking powder

½ tsp. table salt

¾ cup milk

1 tsp. vanilla extract

1 Tbsp. unsweetened cocoa, divided

1½ tsp. red food coloring

1½ tsp. green food coloring

Snowy White Vanilla Glaze (recipe follows)

Fresh mint sprigs, red-and-white fondant balls, for garnish (optional)

1. Preheat oven to 325°F. Beat butter with a heavy-duty electric stand mixer on medium speed until creamy. Gradually add sugar, beating until light and fluffy. Add eggs, 1 at a time, beating just until blended after each addition.

2. Stir together flour, and baking powder, salt. Add to butter mixture alternately with milk, beginning and ending with flour mixture. Beat on low speed just until blended after each addition. Stir in vanilla. Transfer 1¼ cups plain batter to a small bowl; stir in 1½ teaspoons cocoa and the 1½ teaspoons red food coloring. Transfer 1¼ cups plain batter to second small bowl; stir in remaining 1½ teaspoons cocoa and the 1½ teaspoons green food coloring.

3. Drop 2 scoops of plain batter into a greased and floured 10-inch (16-cup) Bundt pan, using a small cookie scoop (about 1½ inches); top with 1 scoop of red velvet batter, 1 scoop of plain batter, 1 scoop of green velvet batter. Repeat around entire pan, covering bottom completely. Continue layering batters in pan as directed until all batter is used.

4. Bake in preheated oven until a long wooden pick inserted in center comes out clean, about 1 hour. Cool in pan on a wire rack 10 minutes; remove from pan to a wire rack, and cool completely (about 1 hour). Drizzle with Snowy White Vanilla Glaze. Garnish with mint and fondant, if desired.

Snowy White Vanilla Glaze: Whisk together 2½ cups powdered sugar, 3 Tbsp. plus 1 tsp. milk, and 1 tsp. vanilla extract until smooth. **Makes about 1 cup**

Lemon-Coconut Cake

SERVES 12 ACTIVE 30 MIN. TOTAL 50 MIN.

This classic layer cake features a tangy lemon filling between layers of tender white cake and a rich coconut-cream cheese frosting.

1 cup butter, softened

2 cups granulated sugar

4 large eggs, separated

3 cups all-purpose flour

1 Tbsp. baking powder

1 cup milk

1 tsp. vanilla extract

Lemon Filling (recipe follows)

Cream Cheese Frosting (recipe follows)

2 cups sweetened flaked coconut, toasted

Lemon slices, for garnish (optional)

1. Preheat oven to 350°F. Beat butter with an electric mixer on medium speed until fluffy; gradually add sugar, beating well. Add egg yolks, 1 at a time, beating until blended after each addition.

2. Combine flour and baking powder; add to butter mixture alternately with milk, beginning and ending with flour mixture. Beat on low speed until blended after each addition. Stir in vanilla.

3. Beat egg whites with electric mixer on high speed until stiff peaks form; fold one-third of egg whites into batter. Gently fold in remaining beaten egg whites just until blended. Spoon batter into 3 greased and floured 9-inch round cake pans.

4. Bake in preheated oven until a wooden pick inserted in center comes out clean, 18 to 20 minutes. Cool in pans on wire racks 10 minutes; remove from pans. Cool completely on wire racks.

5. Spread Lemon Filling between cake layers. Spread Cream Cheese Frosting on top and sides of cake. Sprinkle top and sides with coconut. Garnish, if desired.

Lemon Filling

1 cup granulated sugar

¼ cup cornstarch

1 cup boiling water

4 egg yolks, lightly beaten

2 tsp. lemon zest

⅓ cup fresh lemon juice

2 Tbsp. butter

1. Combine sugar and cornstarch in a medium saucepan; whisk in boiling water. Cook over medium, whisking constantly, until sugar and cornstarch dissolve (about 2 minutes). Gradually whisk about one-fourth of hot sugar mixture into egg yolks; add to remaining hot sugar mixture in pan, whisking constantly. Whisk in lemon zest and juice.

2. Cook, whisking constantly, until mixture is thickened (2 to 3 minutes). Remove from heat. Whisk in butter; let cool completely, stirring occasionally. **Makes 1⅔ cups**

Cream Cheese Frosting

½ cup butter, softened

1 (8-oz.) pkg. cream cheese, softened

1 (16-oz.) pkg. powdered sugar

1 tsp. vanilla extract

Beat butter and cream cheese with an electric mixer on medium speed until creamy. Gradually add powdered sugar, beating at low speed until blended; stir in vanilla. **Makes about 3 cups**

Orange–Rosemary Cheesecake

CRUST
2½ cups finely crushed crisp almond cookies (from 2 [3.5-oz.] pkg.)

5 Tbsp. butter, melted

2 Tbsp. granulated sugar

CHEESECAKE
5 (8-oz.) pkg. cream cheese, softened

1¾ cups granulated sugar

3 Tbsp. all-purpose flour

5 large eggs

2 large egg yolks

1 Tbsp. orange zest, plus ¼ cup fresh juice (from 1 orange)

1 tsp. vanilla extract

TOPPING
¼ cup orange marmalade (such as Stonewall Kitchen)

1 Tbsp. fresh orange juice

4 oranges, peeled, sliced, and patted dry

Sugared Rosemary (recipe follows)

Fresh winter citrus adds a juicy bright counterpoint to this rich, creamy cheesecake with rosemary and almond notes. You could substitute other citrus varieties, such as grapefruit, tangerine, or blood orange, for the orange here. To keep the cheesecake from getting soggy, arrange the fruit on top just before eating. If you have leftover cheesecake, remove the citrus segments and store separately in the refrigerator.

1. Prepare the Crust: Preheat oven to 325°F. Wrap outside of a lightly greased 9-inch springform pan with heavy-duty aluminum foil. Stir together cookies, butter, and sugar. Press onto bottom and 1 inch up sides of pan. Bake until set, 7 to 8 minutes. Transfer to a wire rack; cool completely, 30 minutes.

2. Prepare the Cheesecake: Beat cream cheese with a heavy-duty stand mixer on medium speed until creamy, 3 minutes. Gradually add sugar and flour, beating until smooth. Add eggs, 1 at a time, beating after each addition. Add egg yolks, 1 at a time, beating after each addition. Beat in zest, juice, and vanilla on low speed just until combined. Pour into prepared pan (it will be full); place on a rimmed baking sheet.

3. Bake in preheated oven until center is almost set but still wobbly, 1 hour and 10 minutes to 1 hour and 20 minutes. Transfer to rack; cool completely, 2 hours. Cover with aluminum foil; chill 8 to 12 hours. Run a knife around outer edge; remove sides of pan.

4. Prepare the Topping: Stir together marmalade and juice in a microwavable bowl. Microwave on HIGH about 45 seconds; stir to make a glaze. Arrange orange slices on Cheesecake; brush with glaze. Garnish with Sugared Rosemary.

Sugared Rosemary: Dip 12 rosemary sprigs in water, then generously sprinkle with 1 cup superfine sugar. Let dry on a parchment- or wax paper–lined baking sheet, about 1 hour.
Makes 12 sprigs

Fudge Cake with Caramel–Bourbon Buttercream

SERVES **16**   ACTIVE **1 HOUR**   TOTAL **3 HOURS, 10 MIN.**

This swoon-worthy layer cake is a chocolate-lovers' dream!

FUDGE CAKE
1½ cups bittersweet chocolate chips

½ cup butter, softened

1 (1-lb.) pkg. light brown sugar

3 large eggs

2 cups all-purpose flour, plus more for pans

1 tsp. baking soda

½ tsp. table salt

½ tsp. ground cinnamon

1 (8-oz.) container sour cream

1 cup hot strong brewed coffee

1 Tbsp. (½ oz.) bourbon

CARAMEL BUTTERCREAM
1 cup granulated sugar

⅓ cup water

⅓ cup heavy cream

¼ cup butter, chilled and cut into ½-inch pieces

1 cup butter, softened

4 oz. cream cheese, softened

½ tsp. vanilla extract

¼ tsp. table salt

4 cups unsifted powdered sugar

CHOCOLATE GANACHE
8 oz. semisweet baking chocolate (2 [4-oz.] baking chocolate bars), chopped

6 oz. bittersweet baking chocolate (from 2 [4-oz.] baking chocolate bars), chopped

1½ cups heavy cream

ADDITIONAL INGREDIENT
Shaved bittersweet chocolate

1. Prepare the Cake: Coat 2 (9-inch) square cake pans with cooking spray; dust with flour. Preheat oven to 350°F. Microwave chocolate chips in a microwavable bowl on MEDIUM (50% power) until melted, about 2 minutes, stopping to stir every 30 seconds. Stir until completely smooth.

2. Beat butter and brown sugar in the bowl of a heavy-duty stand mixer on medium until combined, about 5 minutes. Add eggs, 1 at a time, beating to combine after each addition. Add melted chocolate, beating until just combined.

3. Sift together flour, baking soda, salt, and cinnamon. Gradually add to chocolate mixture alternately with sour cream, beginning and ending with flour mixture, beating on low speed to blend after each addition. Gradually add coffee, beating on low. Stir in bourbon. Pour batter evenly into prepared pans.

4. Bake cake layers in preheated oven until a wooden pick comes out clean, 22 to 25 minutes. Cool in pans on wire racks 10 minutes. Remove cake layers from pans; transfer to wire racks to cool completely, about 1 hour.

5. Prepare the Buttercream: Place sugar and water in a saucepan; cook, stirring, over medium-high, until sugar dissolves, about 1 minute. Bring to a boil over medium-high. Cook, without stirring but swirling pan occasionally, until deep amber, about 10 minutes. Remove from heat. Add cream in a steady stream, stirring constantly. Stir in chilled butter until smooth; transfer to a bowl to cool, about 1 hour.

6. Beat softened butter and cream cheese in bowl of a heavy-duty stand mixer on medium until creamy, 3 minutes. Stir in vanilla and salt. Add 2 cups of the powdered sugar, beating on low until smooth, 2 minutes. Add caramel; beat on medium until combined, 2 minutes. Beat in remaining 2 cups powdered sugar on low to combine.

7. Prepare the Chocolate Ganache: Microwave semisweet and bittersweet baking chocolates and cream in a microwavable bowl on MEDIUM (50% power) for 1 minute. Remove and stir. Microwave until melted, 3 to 3½ minutes, stopping to stir every 30 seconds.

8. Assemble Cake: Place 1 cake layer on a platter; pour half of ganache on top, allowing some to drip over edges. Freeze to set, about 5 minutes. Spread half of buttercream to edges. Top with remaining layer; repeat with remaining ganache and buttercream. Garnish with shaved chocolate.

Gingerbread Latte Cake with Vanilla Whipped Cream Frosting

If your holiday season officially starts with a gingerbread latte, this is the cake of your coffee-loving dreams. Three layers of spicy gingerbread are brushed with Espresso Simple Syrup and then covered in fluffy Vanilla Whipped Cream Frosting, which provides the perfect snowy backdrop for an array of store-bought (or homemade) gingerbread shapes of your choosing.

CAKE LAYERS

3¾ cups all-purpose flour, plus more for dusting pans

½ cup chopped crystallized ginger

2 tsp. baking powder

1 tsp. baking soda

1 tsp. table salt

1 tsp. ground cinnamon

¼ tsp. ground ginger

¼ tsp. ground nutmeg

1 cup salted butter, softened

1½ cups packed light brown sugar

3 large eggs, separated

1½ cups hot strong brewed coffee

½ cup molasses

Vegetable shortening, for greasing pans

ESPRESSO SIMPLE SYRUP

¾ cup hot very strong brewed coffee

½ cup granulated sugar

VANILLA WHIPPED CREAM FROSTING

3 cups heavy cream

1½ tsp. vanilla bean paste

½ cup granulated sugar

ADDITIONAL INGREDIENTS

Prepared gingerbread cookie shapes

1. Prepare the Cake Layers: Preheat oven to 350°F. Process flour and next 7 ingredients in a food processor until crystallized ginger is finely ground, about 1 minute. Set aside.

2. Beat butter with a heavy-duty electric stand mixer on medium speed until creamy. Gradually add brown sugar, beating until light and fluffy. Add egg yolks, 1 at a time, beating just until blended after each addition. Stir together coffee and molasses in a glass measuring cup. Add flour mixture to butter mixture alternately with coffee mixture, beginning and ending with flour mixture, beating on low speed just until blended after each addition.

3. Place egg whites in a bowl. Beat with an electric mixer on high speed until stiff peaks form. Gently fold egg whites, in thirds, into batter, folding just until incorporated after each addition.

4. Spoon batter into 3 greased (with vegetable shortening) and floured 9-inch round cake pans. Bake in preheated oven until a wooden pick inserted in center of cakes comes out clean, 19 to 22 minutes.

5. Meanwhile, prepare the Espresso Simple Syrup: Bring coffee and sugar to a boil in a small saucepan over medium-high. Boil, stirring occasionally, until reduced to about ½ cup, 5 to 6 minutes.

6. Remove cakes from oven, and cool in pans on wire racks 10 minutes. Transfer from pans to wire racks; brush evenly with warm Espresso Simple Syrup. Cool completely, about 1 hour.

7. Prepare the Vanilla Whipped Cream Frosting: While Cake Layers cool, beat cream and vanilla bean paste with an electric mixer on medium speed until foamy, 1 to 2 minutes. Gradually add sugar, beating until stiff peaks form, about 2 minutes. (Do not overbeat.)

8. Assemble the Cake: Spread frosting between layers and on top and sides of cake. Arrange gingerbread cookie shapes around the bottom of the cake to create a festive holiday scene.

Snacktastic!

This season of giving shouldn't break the bank. Homemade snacks from the kitchen are a delicious and economical way to check everyone off your list. Satisfy salt-cravers with a nut mix, flavorful popcorn blend, savory shortbread, or a bundle of homemade potato chips paired with a jar of caviar. What sweet tooth can resist decorated sugar cookies, festive gingerbread, or Southern pecan cookies? We haven't met one yet.

ROSEMARY-BACON NUT MIX   SMOKED GOUDA SHORTBREAD
WITH VARIATIONS   ZESTY PARMESAN POPCORN   CRISPY POTATO CHIPS
WITH CAVIAR   ICED SUGAR COOKIES WITH VARIATIONS

Rosemary-Bacon Nut Mix

SERVES **12**   ACTIVE **15 MIN.**   TOTAL **1 HOUR**

Sometimes you feel like a nut, and sometimes you crave something fruity. The raisins in this addictive mix add just the right note of sweet to the savory.

2 Tbsp. finely chopped fresh rosemary

1 Tbsp. dark brown sugar

1 tsp. kosher salt

1/2 tsp. cayenne pepper

6 oz. thick-cut bacon (about 5 slices)

1 1/2 cups (7 oz.) raw cashews

1 1/2 cups (6 oz.) raw pecan halves

1 cup (5 oz.) raw almonds

1/2 cup golden raisins

1 Tbsp. soy sauce

1. Preheat oven to 350°F. Line a baking sheet with parchment paper. Stir together rosemary, brown sugar, salt, and cayenne pepper in a small bowl. Set aside.

2. Cook bacon in a large skillet over medium, turning occasionally, until crisp, 14 to 18 minutes. Transfer bacon to a plate lined with paper towels; reserve for another use. Pour drippings through a fine-mesh strainer into a bowl; discard solids. Wipe skillet clean.

3. Heat 3 tablespoons of the drippings in the skillet over medium. Add cashews, pecan halves, almonds, raisins, soy sauce, and rosemary mixture. Cook, stirring often, until nuts are coated and sugar has melted, 2 to 4 minutes. Spread the nuts on the prepared baking sheet in a single layer. Bake in preheated oven until toasted, stirring occasionally, 10 to 14 minutes. Cool completely, 30 minutes. Store in an airtight container up to 1 week.

Smoked Gouda Shortbread

MAKES **ABOUT 50**   ACTIVE **20 MIN.**   TOTAL **2 HOURS**

8 oz. smoked Gouda cheese, finely shredded (about 2 cups)

1 cup all-purpose flour

1/2 cup fine plain white cornmeal

1 Tbsp. cornstarch

1/2 tsp. kosher salt

1/2 tsp. dry mustard

1/4 tsp. black pepper

1/2 cup cold unsalted butter, cut into 1/2-inch pieces

1. Process cheese and next 6 ingredients in a food processor until combined, about 5 seconds. Add butter, and process until mixture resembles wet sand, about 20 seconds. With processor running, add 3 tablespoons water through food chute; process until dough forms a ball, 10 to 15 seconds.

2. Divide dough in half, and shape each half into a 6-inch log, about 1¾ inches in diameter. Wrap logs individually in plastic wrap; chill at least 1 hour or up to 2 days.

3. Preheat oven to 350°F with oven racks in upper and lower thirds. Unwrap logs; slice into 1/8-inch-thick rounds. Place 1/2 inch apart, on 2 parchment paper-lined baking sheets.

4. Bake in preheated oven until edges are golden, 14 minutes, rotating baking sheets halfway through bake time. Cool on baking sheets 5 minutes. Transfer to a wire rack; cool completely.

Pimiento Cheese Shortbread

Prepare recipe as directed in Step 1, substituting finely shredded sharp cheddar cheese for the smoked Gouda. Knead 1/4 cup diced well-drained pimientos and 1/4 cup chopped fresh chives into dough. Proceed with recipe as directed in Steps 2 through 4.

Pecan-and-Thyme Shortbread

Prepare recipe as directed in Step 1, substituting finely shredded sharp cheddar cheese for the smoked Gouda. Knead 1/2 cup finely chopped toasted pecans and 1½ Tbsp. chopped fresh thyme into dough. Proceed with recipe as directed in Steps 2 through 4.

Bacon, Bourbon, and Benne Seed Shortbread

Prepare recipe as directed in Step 1, substituting finely shredded sharp white cheddar cheese for the smoked Gouda, adding 1 Tbsp. dark brown sugar with cheese mixture, and substituting bourbon for water. Knead ½ cup chopped cooked bacon into dough. Proceed with recipe as directed in Steps 2 and 3, rolling dough logs in ⅓ cup benne (sesame) seeds before wrapping and chilling. Just before baking, sprinkle 2 Tbsp. benne seeds evenly over dough rounds. Proceed as directed in Step 4.

Zesty Parmesan Popcorn

SERVES 12   ACTIVE 15 MIN.   TOTAL 15 MIN.

Perfect for movie night munching or for giving, this popcorn recipe can be tailored to what you like or have on hand. Replace the Parmesan with Pecorino or Asiago, and use fresh rosemary or thyme in place of the oregano.

¼ cup extra-virgin olive oil

1 Tbsp. minced garlic (about 3 garlic cloves)

2 tsp. finely chopped fresh oregano

2 Tbsp. canola oil

⅓ cup popcorn kernels

½ cup grated Parmesan cheese

¼ tsp. fine sea salt

1. Place extra-virgin olive oil and minced garlic in a small saucepan; heat over medium-low, undisturbed, until sizzling, about 2 minutes. Reduce heat to low. Add oregano; stir once, and cook, undisturbed, until garlic softens and oregano is fragrant, about 2 minutes. Remove from heat.

2. Place canola oil in a large saucepan fitted with a lid; heat over high. Add 2 popcorn kernels, and cover and shake saucepan until kernels pop, 2 to 3 minutes. Add remaining popcorn kernels, and cover and shake constantly until kernels stop popping, about 2 minutes. Immediately pour into a large bowl. Drizzle with garlic-oregano oil, stirring to coat. Add Parmesan and sea salt; toss to coat. Serve immediately, or cool and store in an air tight container.

Crispy Potato Chips with Caviar

SERVES 6   ACTIVE 25 MIN.   TOTAL 40 MIN.

Yes, you could buy your favorite potato chips to bundle up for this high-low chips-and-caviar gift, but the delicate crunch of homemade chips makes it worth the extra effort. The key is to slice potatoes as thinly as possible. A mandoline makes easy work of it.

2 large russet potatoes (about 2¼ lb.)

2 Tbsp. white vinegar

Peanut oil

1 Tbsp. freshly ground black pepper

Kosher salt

Jar of Southern caviar

Sour cream and sliced fresh chives, for garnish

1. Cut potatoes into thin slices, using a mandoline or sharp knife; rinse with cold water.

2. Bring vinegar and 6 cups water to a boil in a large saucepan over high heat. Add sliced potatoes, and cook 3 minutes. Drain potatoes, and spread on a paper towel-lined baking sheet. Pat dry with paper towels, and chill 15 minutes.

3. Meanwhile, pour oil to a depth of 3 inches into a large Dutch oven, and heat to 340°F. Fry potatoes, in batches, stirring occasionally, 3 to 4 minutes or until golden brown. Drain on paper towels, and immediately sprinkle with black pepper and desired amount of kosher salt. Serve with caviar, sour cream, and chives.

Look for these deliciously sustainable caviars from Southern waters that can be purchased online and in fine grocery stores.

1. Cajun Caviar American Bowfin Caviar (Louisiana)

2. Sunburst Trout Farms Smoked Rainbow Trout Caviar (North Carolina)

3. America's Best Caviar Hackleback Caviar (Kentucky)

4. Kelley Katch Paddlefish Caviar (Tennessee)

Iced Sugar Cookies

MAKES **40 COOKIES**   ACTIVE **45 MIN.**
TOTAL **3 HOURS, 12 MIN.**

COOKIES

9 oz. all-purpose flour (2 cups)

½ tsp. salt

¼ tsp. baking powder

¾ cup butter

⅔ cup granulated sugar

1 large egg

1½ tsp. vanilla extract

ICING

1½ cups powdered sugar

4 tsp. egg white powder

⅛ tsp. salt

2 Tbsp. water

Sparkling sugar (optional)

Add water to icing a drop at a time for thinner spreading consistency. Decorate with dragée (sometimes called sugar pearls), gold or silver dust, and coarse or sparkling sugar, and tint the frosting with food color paste. Make the cookie dough up to a month in advance, wrap it tightly, and freeze. Thaw dough completely by placing it in the refrigerator overnight.

1. Preheat oven to 350°F.

2. Prepare the Cookies. Spoon flour into dry measuring cups, and level with a knife. Combine flour, salt, and baking powder in a small bowl, stirring with a whisk. Place butter and sugar in a large bowl, and beat with a mixer on high speed until light and fluffy. Add egg, and beat until well blended. Beat in vanilla. Add the flour mixture to butter mixture; beat on low speed just until combined.

3. Shape dough into a 4-inch round, and cover with plastic wrap. Chill for 1 hour. Roll dough to ¼-inch thickness on a lightly floured surface. Cut out 40 (2- to 3-inch) cookies, rerolling scraps as necessary. Place cookies 1 inch apart on a baking sheet lined with parchment paper. Bake in preheated oven until lightly browned on bottoms, about 9 minutes. Cool on a wire rack.

4. Prepare the Icing. Combine powdered sugar, egg white powder, and ⅛ teaspoon salt in a medium bowl, stirring well. Gradually add the water, stirring constantly with a whisk until smooth. Decorate cookies as desired. Sprinkle with sparkling sugar, if desired. Let cookies stand on wire rack until icing is completely dry (about 1 hour).

Gingerbread Cookies

Prepare Iced Sugar Cookies, increasing flour to 11.25 ounces (about 2½ cups). Stir 1 tablespoon ground ginger, 1 teaspoon ground cinnamon, ½ teaspoon ground cloves, and ¼ teaspoon ground allspice into flour mixture. Add ¼ cup molasses to dough when vanilla is added. Halve icing recipe; decorate as desired. **Makes 40 cookies**

Tip: Flourishes don't require special equipment. First, "flood" cookies by spreading thin frosting with a small offset spatula to coat, if desired. Pipe thicker frosting from a zip-top bag to outline. Use a toothpick to make small dots of icing that act as glue for decorative details like sugar pearls.

Pecan Cookies

Prepare Iced Sugar Cookies, decreasing the butter to 10 tablespoons. Stir ¾ cup chopped toasted pecans into dough. Omit icing. Place ⅓ cup powdered sugar in a fine sieve; shake over cooled cookies. **Makes 40 cookies**

The Scoop on Perfect Sugar Cookies

Choose Wisely: Pick a baking sheet that allows 2 inches of clearance on all sides of the oven. This will allow for good air circulation and even baking.

Stock Up: Always have two or three baking sheets on hand. Reusing the same sheet over and over will make your subsequent batches melt.

Cut Corners: Line your pan with parchment that hangs over the sides so it's easy to lift cookies out and clean the pan.

Flip It: You can reuse your custom-cut parchment sheet by simply turning it over.

Shape Up: Choose cookie cutters with simple shapes; they're easier to handle and the cookies are less likely to break. Make sure to flour the cutter before using to prevent the dough from sticking to it.

Switch It Up: Cut-out cookies don't have to be vanilla. This year, try a deep, dark chocolate version. Dust the cutting board with cocoa powder for color and flavor.

Reach for a Spoon: When measuring flour, spoon—don't pack—the dry ingredient into the measuring cup. This technique helps yield tender cookies.

Crack the Right Eggs: You'll want to bake with room-temperature eggs so they easily incorporate into your dough. In a rush? Just sit them in a bowl of warm tap water for 10 minutes.

Roll It Right: We think ⅛ inch is the perfect thickness for a crisp, buttery cookie, but this dough can be rolled to ¼ inch thick if you prefer a soft texture.

Make a Little Noise: When cookies are done, sharply tap the baking sheet against the counter. It will force the cookies to settle faster, creating a crisp outside and a chewy center.

Travel Lightly: Delicate or intricately shaped cookies aren't built for traveling. Slice-and-bake or drop cookies are more durable and more likely to survive the journey.

Thanks to these vendors

We wish to thank the following vendors and resources whose products were photographed on the pages of this book.

Accent Décor

Albin Hagstrom & Son, Inc.

Ballard Designs

Black Bough

Crate & Barrel

Creative Co-op

eBay

Etsy

Factory Direct Craft

Hobby Lobby

HomArt

Home Goods

Houses and Parties

Julie Terrell

LaRibbons & Crafts

Lion Ribbon

Michaels Stores

Pastiche Studios

OK Flower Market Wholesale Florist

Overstock

Park Hill Collection

Sister Parish

Sorghum Hill

Target

Tinsel Trading

Trader Joe's

Tuesday Morning

Violet Rose Living

Special thanks to these small businesses, shops, artisans, and restaurants.

ALKMY
(Mountain Brook, AL)

Bess Booth Calligraphy
(Birmingham, AL)

Christmas Expressions
(Norman, OK)

Davis Wholesale Florist
(Birmingham, AL)

The General
(Birmingham, AL)

Gilchrist (Mountain Brook, AL)

Hall's Birmingham Wholesale Florist
(Birmingham, AL)

Leaf & Petal
(Mountain Brook, AL)

The Merriment Mill – Megann Frazier
(Edmond, OK)

Oak Street Garden Shop
(Mountain Brook, AL)

Paige Albright Orientals
(Mountain Brook, AL)

Prisem Art Studio
(Norman, OK)

Quincy Bakeshop
(Oklahoma City, OK)

Shoppe (Birmingham, AL)

Thanks to the following individuals and venues for allowing us to photograph in their spaces.

Sara Kate & Jason Little

Bradford House

Jan Miller

General Index

M

Magnolia

in arrangements, 30–31, 61

caring for arrangements, 54

in garland, 56–57

terrace decorations, 28–29

mantel decorations, 21

Menus

Appalachian Breakfast Board, The, 68–71

Christmas Day Buffet, 96–105

Creole Brunch Board, The, 72–75

Delta Dessert Board, The, 80–83

Floribbean Sunset Board, The, 76–79

Morning Glories, 106–111

Merriment Mill, The, 30

Metric charts, 172

Miller, Jan, 36, 38, 41, 43, 45, 46, 48, 50

Moravian star light, 44–45

Morning Glories, 106–111

N

notes for next year, 192

November calendar, 178–179

O

one-dish dinners, 84–95

Ornaments

color scheme, 18, 19

reading light decorations, 46

Shiny Brite, 22–23

Outdoor decorations

backyard, 48–49

terrace, decorating a, 28–29

urns, 36

oven-to-slow cooker conversions, 116

P

paperwhites, 46

Pastiche Studios, 25

Patrick Baty's Papers and Paints, 21

peonies, 27, 30

pepperberry, 16, 27

Pie for the Course, 136–145

pine and rosemary wreaths, 60–61

pine cones, 58

plate racks, 40–41

plates, warming, in slow cooker, 94

poinsettias, 46

Q

Quincy Bakeshop, 30

R

rosemary wreaths, 60–61

S

sheet pans, caring for, 90

Shiny Brite ornaments, 22–23

Side Ways, 127–135

Sister Parish fabrics, 26, 27

slow cooker, warming plates in, 94

Snacktastic!, 158–167

staircases, 16, 17

Stockings

for children, 44–45

evergreen tassel for, 61

Sister Parish fabrics, 26–27

storage shed, 48–49

T

Table scape

bouquets, 58–59

outdoor dining, 50–51

place settings, 50

Take a Bough, 52–63

Take the Cake, 146–157

tassels, 16–17

thank-you note checklist, 192

V

vendors, 169

W

Wreaths

boxwood, 42–43

evergreen, 28–29

indoor decorations, 42–43

outside doors, 48–49, 55

petite-size, 60–61

ribbon embellishments, 21

silk sash hanger for, 24–25

window decorations, 42–43

Metric Charts

The recipes that appear in this cookbook use the standard US method for measuring liquid and dry or solid ingredients (teaspoons, tablespoons, and cups). The information on these pages is provided to help cooks outside the United States successfully use these recipes. All equivalents are approximate.

Metric Equivalents for Different Types of Ingredients

A standard cup measure of a dry or solid ingredient will vary in weight depending on the type of ingredient. A standard cup of liquid is the same volume for any type of liquid. Use the following chart when converting standard cup measures to grams (weight) or milliliters (volume).

STANDARD CUP	FINE POWDER (ex. flour)	GRAIN (ex. rice)	GRANULAR (ex. sugar)	LIQUID SOLIDS (ex. butter)	LIQUID (ex. milk)
1	140 g	150 g	190 g	200 g	240 ml
3/4	105 g	113 g	143 g	150 g	180 ml
2/3	93 g	100 g	125 g	133 g	160 ml
1/2	70 g	75 g	95 g	100 g	120 ml
1/3	47 g	50 g	63 g	67 g	80 ml
1/4	35 g	38 g	48 g	50 g	60 ml
1/8	18 g	19 g	24 g	25 g	30 ml

Useful Equivalents for Liquid Ingredients by Volume

TSP	TBSP	CUPS	FL OZ	ML	L
1/4 tsp				1 ml	
1/2 tsp				2 ml	
1 tsp				5 ml	
3 tsp	1 Tbsp		1/2 fl oz	15 ml	
	2 Tbsp	1/8 cup	1 fl oz	30 ml	
	4 Tbsp	1/4 cup	2 fl oz	60 ml	
	5 1/3 Tbsp	1/3 cup	3 fl oz	80 ml	
	8 Tbsp	1/2 cup	4 fl oz	120 ml	
	10 2/3 Tbsp	2/3 cup	5 fl oz	160 ml	
	12 Tbsp	3/4 cup	6 fl oz	180 ml	
	16 Tbsp	1 cup	8 fl oz	240 ml	
	1 pt	2 cups	16 fl oz	480 ml	
	1 qt	4 cups	32 fl oz	960 ml	
			33 fl oz	1000 ml	1 L

Useful Equivalents for Dry Ingredients by Weight

(To convert ounces to grams, multiply the number of ounces by 30.)

OZ	LB	G
1 oz	1/16 lb	30 g
4 oz	1/4 lb	120 g
8 oz	1/2 lb	240 g
12 oz	3/4 lb	360 g
16 oz	1 lb	480 g

Useful Equivalents for Length

(To convert inches to centimeters, multiply the number of inches by 2.5.)

IN	FT	YD	CM	M
1 in			2.5 cm	
6 in	1/2 ft		15 cm	
12 in	1 ft		30 cm	
36 in	3 ft	1 yd	90 cm	
40 in			100 cm	1 m

Useful Equivalents for Cooking/Oven Temperatures

	FAHRENHEIT	CELSIUS	GAS MARK
FREEZE WATER	32°F	0°C	
ROOM TEMPERATURE	68°F	20°C	
BOIL WATER	212°F	100°C	
	325°F	160°C	3
	350°F	180°C	4
	375°F	190°C	5
	400°F	200°C	6
	425°F	220°C	7
	450°F	230°C	8
BROIL			Grill

Recipe Index

MEREDITH CONSUMER MARKETING
Direct Marketing-Books: Daniel Fagan
Marketing Operations Manager: Max Daily
Assistant Marketing Manager: Kylie Dazzo
Content Manager: Julie Doll
Marketing Coordinator: Elizabeth Moore
Senior Production Manager: Liza Ward

PRODUCED BY:
BLUELINE CREATIVE GROUP LLC
visit: bluelinecreativegroup.com
Executive Producer/Editor: Katherine Cobbs
Art Director: Matt Ryan
Location Photographers: Robbie Caponetto, Emily Hart, Laurey W. Glenn
Location Photo Assistant: Hanna Runner
Location Stylists: Buffy Hargett Miller, Kathleen Varner, Sara Gae Waters

STUDIO RECIPE PHOTOGRAPHY:
MEREDITH FOOD STUDIOS
Director: Allison Lowery
Photography Director: Sheri Wilson
Photographer: Antonis Achilleos
Prop Stylists: Kay E. Clarke, Buffy Hargett Miller
Food Stylists: Margaret Monroe Dickey, Emily Nabors Hall, Ali Ramee

PRINT PRODUCTION:
WATERBURY PUBLICATIONS, INC.

Library of Congress Control Number: 2022932875

ISBN-13: 978-1-4197-6387-8

First Edition 2022
Printed in the United States of America
10 9 8 7 6 5 4 3 2 1
Call 1-800-826-4707 for more information

Distributed in 2022 by Abrams, an imprint of ABRAMS.
Abrams® is a registered trademark of Harry N. Abrams, Inc.

ABRAMS The Art of Books
195 Broadway, New York, NY 10007
abramsbooks.com

Holiday Planner

Get a jump-start on your holiday to-do list with this helpful planner. Create guest lists, keep track of gifts for family and friends, and stay on top of all the details for an organized, low-stress holiday.

November 2022

SUNDAY	MONDAY	TUESDAY	WEDNESDAY
		Send Thanksgiving invites, plan menu, and create shopping list. **1**	Get the house guest-ready. Tackle repairs and tidy up. **2**
Daylight saving time ends. Turn clocks back for an extra hour of rest! **6**	Set out serving pieces you plan to use. Attach sticky notes with what will go in each. **7**	Take inventory of pots, pans, and baking dishes. Buy or borrow any needed. **8**	Plan your centerpiece and table setting. **9**
Clean out, wipe down, and organize the fridge. **13**	Buy nonperishables in bulk to save on pricier items like nuts and dried fruit. **14**	Tidy the least-used rooms in the house, which are less likely to get messy again. **15**	Round up board games, playing cards, and photo albums to entertain guests while you're busy in the kitchen. **16**
Throwing a holiday party? Get invites out now. Calendars fill up fast! **20**	Serving a frozen turkey? Allow one day to thaw in the fridge for every 4 pounds of bird. **21**	Create space in the coat closet, and vacuum and dust the entry. **22**	Create a festive holiday playlist. Buy fresh flowers and other perishables needed and assemble centerpiece. **23**
Time to start thinking Christmas! Enjoy more Thanksgiving leftovers. **27**	If you prefer online shopping, start clicking! Cyber Monday is here. **28**	Create a holiday playlist. **29**	Gather recipes, plan Christmas menus (page 64), and clip coupons. **30**

THURSDAY	FRIDAY	SATURDAY
Light a gingerbread or pine candle to get in the holiday spirit.	Request gift ideas now and start your holiday shopping early.	Serving fresh turkey for Thanksgiving? Order now.
3	**4**	**5**
Get holiday cards and start your list (page 189).	Confirm head count for Thanksgiving dinner.	Need a kids' table? Cover a small table with craft paper and provide crayons.
10	**11**	**12**
Iron linens you plan to use and polish the silver.	Make a prep list for each dish. Draw up a daily plan from now through Thanksgiving Day to spread tasks out.	Shop for perishable grocery items such as milk, cheese, and produce.
17	**18**	**19**
Happy Thanksgiving! Say "yes" to offers of help from guests so you can enjoy the day.	Shoppers, start your engines— it's Black Friday!	Enjoy those Thanksgiving leftovers.
Thanksgiving **24**	**25**	**26**

Holiday Hotlines

Use these toll-free numbers when you have last-minute food questions.

USDA Meat & Poultry Hotline: 1-888-674-6854

FDA Center for Food Safety: 1-888-723-3366

Butterball Turkey Talk-Line: 1-800-288-8372

December 2022

SUNDAY	MONDAY	TUESDAY	WEDNESDAY
Get crafty. Plan homemade gifts (page 188) and decorating projects (page 182). **4**	Make cookie dough and freeze, or bake cookies and cakes and freeze unfrosted. **5**	Send out holiday cards. Don't wait until post office lines grow. **6**	Give back: Find volunteer opportunities, donate food or gifts, or deliver meals. **7**
Trim the tree, hang wreaths, display cards, and dust off Christmas accents. The sooner you finish, the longer you can enjoy them. **11**	Make a gingerbread house! **12**	Wrap holiday gifts. **13**	Bake and decorate holiday cookies. **14**
Bundle up and head out to enjoy the Christmas lights. **18**	Take a break and treat yourself to a hot bath, coffee with a friend, or a nap. **19**	Watch your favorite holiday film by a roaring fire. **20**	It's the first day of winter—days will get longer! **21**
Merry Christmas! Enjoy a Christmas Day Buffet (page 96). **Christmas 25**	Indulge in a sweet treat before resolutions kick in (page 146). **Boxing Day 26**	Having a NYE Party? Make a festive food board (page 66) **27**	Phone loved ones you missed this holiday. **28**

THURSDAY	FRIDAY	SATURDAY
Set up firewood delivery.	Test the Christmas lights and replace fuses or strands.	Organize gift wrap, cards, ribbons, tape, and scissors.
1	**2**	**3**
Gather unused gift cards and check expirations. Use them to buy gifts for others.	Dehydrate citrus slices in a low oven for pretty ornaments or cocktail garnishes.	Pick out your fresh tree or put up the faux fir.
8	**9**	**10**
Keep your Christmas tree fresh and hydrated. Replenish water pan daily.	Acknowledge those who brighten your day—teacher, mail carrier, babysitter, favorite colleague—with a small gift.	Finalize online purchases today before shipping prices jump.
15	**16**	**17**
Simmer cloves, allspice, an apple, and a cinnamon stick in water to festively scent your home.	Organize the stocking stuffers.	Gather loved ones for a Game Night (page 84).
22	**23**	**24**
Return or exchange any gifts before return deadlines.	Write thank-you notes.	Toast 2023 with family, friends, and loved ones!
29	**30**	**New Year's Eve 31**

Decorating Planner

Here's a list of details and finishing touches you can use to
tailor a picture-perfect house this holiday season.

Decorative materials needed

FROM THE YARD ....

FROM AROUND THE HOUSE ....

FROM THE STORE ....

OTHER ....

Holiday decorations

FOR THE TABLE ....

FOR THE DOOR ....

FOR THE MANTEL ....

FOR THE STAIRCASE ....

OTHER ....

Create a Decorator's Toolkit

Our photo stylists guard their toolkits like the family jewels. A well-stocked kit means
you have just what you need at the ready to get you through the holidays and beyond.

- ☐ Tools (hammer, screwdrivers, clamps)
- ☐ Nails, screws, s-hooks, tacks
- ☐ Adhesive strips and hooks
- ☐ Staple gun and staples
- ☐ Hot-glue gun and glue sticks
- ☐ Craft glue
- ☐ Super glue
- ☐ Clothespins
- ☐ Funnel
- ☐ Tape measure
- ☐ Twine

- ☐ Fishing line
- ☐ Green floralists wire
- ☐ Sewing kit
- ☐ Lint roller
- ☐ Steamer or iron
- ☐ Paintbrushes (assorted)
- ☐ Scissors
- ☐ Floralists snips
- ☐ Lighter
- ☐ Batteries (assorted)
- ☐ Fuses for Christmas lights
- ☐ Clear tape

- ☐ Double-sided tape
- ☐ Painters tape
- ☐ Clear mounting wax
- ☐ Putty
- ☐ Adhesive remover
- ☐ Lubricant spray
- ☐ Window cleaner
- ☐ Furniture polish
- ☐ Touch-up paint
- ☐ Static duster
- ☐ Stain stick

From Grocery Store to Gorgeous

Decking the halls can be as easy and convenient as a trip to the supermarket for a few staples. Everyday ingredients can be incorporated into creative displays for pennies on the dollar.

Rosemary

Fill your home with the woodsy beauty and distinct fragrance of this fresh herb.

Trim a tabletop rosemary tree. A topiary is a great present that lasts all year, offering tender shoots of herbs that you can add to your favorite recipes.

Gather an evergreen bouquet. A swag of rosemary branches hung on the front door adds Christmas cheer and a fresh aroma as guests come and go.

Adorn gifts with sprigs of fresh rosemary by entwining a fragrant sprig within the ribbon.

Citrus

Add some sunshine to your holiday decor with a favorite fruit of wintertime.

Trim a fruit tree and make it the focal point on your table display. Tie satin bows around its trunk and surround it with other types of citrus for a fresh, abundant display.

Make citrus pomanders by studding citrus varieties with cloves in interesting patterns. Hang the decorated fruit on both Christmas tree and garland for color and scent.

Forgo flowers and turn to citrus for easy long-lasting centerpieces. Fill in the gaps with greenery, or add a lime or two to amplify the green effect.

Cranberries

Very merry berries add a splash of color all through the house.

Freeze fresh cranberries to use in place of ice cubes in drinks to keep them chilled without diluting.

Thread a large needle with clear fishing line, and string fresh cranberries to make a garland. Drape the finished product on the Christmas tree on top of greenery on the mantel.

Use cranberries as colorful "mulch" on top of the soil of small houseplants to add some holiday flair in unexpected places.

Plant an amaryllis bulb in a narrow glass vase. Carefully place the narrow vase inside a larger one, filling the empty space between the two with cranberries.

Fill a canning jar with water and tuck in a few rosemary sprigs for a bit of green. Add a floating candle and surround it with a handful of cranberries for a festive flickering votive.

Party Planner

Stay on top of your party plans with this time-saving menu organizer.

GUESTS	WHAT THEY'RE BRINGING	SERVING PIECES NEEDED
....	☐ appetizer ☐ beverage ☐ bread ☐ main dish ☐ side dish ☐ dessert	....
....	☐ appetizer ☐ beverage ☐ bread ☐ main dish ☐ side dish ☐ dessert	....
....	☐ appetizer ☐ beverage ☐ bread ☐ main dish ☐ side dish ☐ dessert	....
....	☐ appetizer ☐ beverage ☐ bread ☐ main dish ☐ side dish ☐ dessert	....
....	☐ appetizer ☐ beverage ☐ bread ☐ main dish ☐ side dish ☐ dessert	....
....	☐ appetizer ☐ beverage ☐ bread ☐ main dish ☐ side dish ☐ dessert	....
....	☐ appetizer ☐ beverage ☐ bread ☐ main dish ☐ side dish ☐ dessert	....
....	☐ appetizer ☐ beverage ☐ bread ☐ main dish ☐ side dish ☐ dessert	....
....	☐ appetizer ☐ beverage ☐ bread ☐ main dish ☐ side dish ☐ dessert	....
....	☐ appetizer ☐ beverage ☐ bread ☐ main dish ☐ side dish ☐ dessert	....
....	☐ appetizer ☐ beverage ☐ bread ☐ main dish ☐ side dish ☐ dessert	....
....	☐ appetizer ☐ beverage ☐ bread ☐ main dish ☐ side dish ☐ dessert	....
....	☐ appetizer ☐ beverage ☐ bread ☐ main dish ☐ side dish ☐ dessert	....
....	☐ appetizer ☐ beverage ☐ bread ☐ main dish ☐ side dish ☐ dessert	....
....	☐ appetizer ☐ beverage ☐ bread ☐ main dish ☐ side dish ☐ dessert	....
....	☐ appetizer ☐ beverage ☐ bread ☐ main dish ☐ side dish ☐ dessert	....

Party Guest List

....
....
....
....
....
....
....
....
....
....
....
....
....
....

Party To-Do List

....
....
....
....
....
....
....
....
....
....
....
....
....

Christmas Dinner Planner

Use this space to create a menu, to-do list, and guest list for your special holiday celebration.

Menu Ideas

Dinner To-Do List

Christmas Dinner Guest List

Pantry List

....
....
....
....
....
....
....
....
....
....
....
....
....
....
....
....
....
....
....
....
....
....
....
....
....
....
....
....
....

Grocery List

....
....
....
....
....
....
....
....
....
....
....
....
....
....
....
....
....
....
....
....
....
....
....
....
....
....
....
....
....

Gifts & Greetings

Keep up with family and friends' sizes, jot down gift ideas, and record purchases in this convenient chart. Also use it to keep track of addresses for your Christmas card list.

Gift List and Size Charts

	GIFT PURCHASED/MADE	SENT

jeans_____ shirt_____ sweater_____ jacket_____ shoes_____ belt_____
blouse_____ skirt_____ slacks_____ dress_____ suit_____ coat_____
pajamas_____ robe_____ hat_____ gloves_____ ring_____

jeans_____ shirt_____ sweater_____ jacket_____ shoes_____ belt_____
blouse_____ skirt_____ slacks_____ dress_____ suit_____ coat_____
pajamas_____ robe_____ hat_____ gloves_____ ring_____

jeans_____ shirt_____ sweater_____ jacket_____ shoes_____ belt_____
blouse_____ skirt_____ slacks_____ dress_____ suit_____ coat_____
pajamas_____ robe_____ hat_____ gloves_____ ring_____

jeans_____ shirt_____ sweater_____ jacket_____ shoes_____ belt_____
blouse_____ skirt_____ slacks_____ dress_____ suit_____ coat_____
pajamas_____ robe_____ hat_____ gloves_____ ring_____

jeans_____ shirt_____ sweater_____ jacket_____ shoes_____ belt_____
blouse_____ skirt_____ slacks_____ dress_____ suit_____ coat_____
pajamas_____ robe_____ hat_____ gloves_____ ring_____

jeans_____ shirt_____ sweater_____ jacket_____ shoes_____ belt_____
blouse_____ skirt_____ slacks_____ dress_____ suit_____ coat_____
pajamas_____ robe_____ hat_____ gloves_____ ring_____

jeans_____ shirt_____ sweater_____ jacket_____ shoes_____ belt_____
blouse_____ skirt_____ slacks_____ dress_____ suit_____ coat_____
pajamas_____ robe_____ hat_____ gloves_____ ring_____

Christmas Card List

NAME	ADDRESS	SENT

Holiday Memories

Hold on to priceless Christmas memories forever with handwritten
recollections of this season's magical moments.

Treasured Traditions

Keep track of your family's favorite holiday customs and pastimes on these lines.

....
....
....
....
....
....
....
....
....
....
....
....

Special Holiday Activities

What holiday events do you look forward to year after year? Write them down here.

....
....
....
....
....
....
....
....
....
....

Holiday Visits and Visitors

Keep a list of this year's holiday visitors.
Jot down friend and family news as well.

....
....
....
....
....
....
....
....
....
....
....
....
....
....
....
....
....
....
....
....
....
....
....
....
....
....
....
....

This Year's Favorite Recipes

APPETIZERS AND BEVERAGES
....
....
....
....

ENTRÉES
....
....
....

SIDES AND SALADS
....
....
....
....

COOKIES AND CANDIES
....
....
....

DESSERTS
....
....
....
....

Looking Ahead

Holiday Wrap-up

Use this checklist to record thank-you notes sent for holiday gifts and hospitality.

NAME	GIFT AND/OR EVENT	NOTE SENT
....	....	☐
....	....	☐
....	....	☐
....	....	☐
....	....	☐
....	....	☐
....	....	☐
....	....	☐
....	....	☐
....	....	☐
....	....	☐
....	....	☐
....	....	☐

Notes for Next Year

Write down your ideas for Christmas 2023 on the lines below.